DECADES

The Sweet

in the 1970s

Darren Johnson

sonicbondpublishing.com

Dedication

This book is dedicated to my late father, Alan Johnson, who
– whether glam, heavy metal, skiffle, blues or rock and roll –
instilled in me a life-long love of music from an early age.

Acknowledgements

A few months ago, I had a vivid dream that I had just written a
book about The Sweet. On waking, I soon realised I had written no
such book but thought it might be a good idea to do so. I emailed
Stephen Lambe that very morning offering to write it and he came
back and said yes. I would like to thank Stephen for giving me that
opportunity. I am indebted to Tracy Dighton, Cheryl Faithful and
Michael Mandt for their comments and to Michael Mandt and
Dean Walton for their assistance with the images.

I would like to thank my partner, friends and family for their
moral support and, finally, I would like to thank Brian Connolly,
Steve Priest, Andy Scott and Mick Tucker for being such an
inspiration to me for all these years.

DECADES | The Sweet in the 1970s

Contents

Foreword

The Sweet's look, sound and attitude became an instantly recognisable hallmark of the early seventies glam rock era. But the band did not start the 1970s as a glam rock band and they certainly did not finish as one. This book charts the band's journey through the decade that made them a household name, from their initial rise as purveyors of disposable, manufactured bubblegum pop to their metamorphosis into harder-edged glam rock icons. And once the sparkle of glam and glitter had begun to pale, we take a look at both their successes and their struggles in their quest to be recognised as a more serious rock act in the latter part of the decade.

The Sweet's prime decade saw them score fifteen UK Top 40 singles, release seven studio albums and tour several continents. Moreover, while their hit singles of the early 1970s strove for commerciality and mass-appeal on the A-sides, the band very rapidly perfected the art of using the B-sides to showcase high-octane, uncompromising, loud and raucous hard rock.

Unlike many other key bands of that decade, personnel changes were few. The Sweet begin the 1970s with the arrival of new guitarist Andy Scott and end them with the departure of frontman Brian Connolly – and an ultimately ill-fated attempt to continue as a three-piece.

The imagery of glam rock bands like The Sweet was striking, outrageous and unforgettable, and remains so to this day. It did not come without consequences later on, however. Problems that dogged perceptions of the band in the second half of the 1970s continued, not just for the rest of the original band's lifetime – going into the start of the 1980s – but for the subsequent decades beyond that, too. For many years virtually any evaluation of the impact of glam would tend to heap praise on the likes of Bolan and Bowie as the pioneers, lavish yet more praise on the art-school protagonists at glam's high-end, like Roxy Music, while the likes of The Sweet would be dismissed as merely jumping on the bandwagon and looking like hod-carriers in make-up. All of that raw excitement and charisma, along with those brilliant, life-enhancing tunes, would be brushed away in a single sentence.

The second edition of the *NME's Book of Rock*, published in 1977 a few years after glam's heyday, is typical. Bowie is lauded as 'one of the most important figures to emerge so far in 1970s rock'. Roxy Music are deemed to have 'warranted all their acclaim as one of Britain's most provocative and entertaining bands.' Sweet, meanwhile, are noted for 'a whole string of instantly catchy, immediately forgettable bubblegum singles.'

Academics and music historians have also been similarly dismissive of what glam had to offer. While the intervening decades saw increased interest in the more art-school, apparently intellectual end of glam, such as the aforementioned Bowie and Roxy Music, there was relatively little written about the likes of The Sweet and Slade. '…critical writing about the more seemingly disposable or disreputable end of glam rock, particularly that aimed at a younger audience – performers such as Marc Bolan or Gary Glitter, or bands such as Slade and The Sweet – is still comparatively hard to find,' wrote Professor David Buckingham in his essay *Glitter, glam and gender play: pop and teenybop in the early 1970s*.

'Glam rock generally is not counted as a significant phenomenon in histories of rock authored by American scholars,' argued Philip Auslander in his 2006 study *Performing Glam Rock: Gender and Theatricality in Popular Music*. 'The conventional narrative is that rock lost its footing in the 1970s… and rediscovered its original energy and impetus only with the advent of punk.'

Over time there have been attempts to redress the balance. Simon Reynolds, in his 2016 publication *Shock and Awe: Glam Rock and its Legacy* attempts to provide a thorough overview of the whole phenomenon of glam rock and its various players. His in-depth study eschews such haughtily dismissive characterisations as 'high glam' and 'low glam'. Even so, a glance at the end pages will reveal that references to David Bowie account for 162 lines of the book's substantial index while just twenty apply to The Sweet.

With the death of bass-player Steve Priest in June 2020, the third of The Sweet's classic foursome to go, we began to see something of a reassessment: an outpouring of love from fans across the world, obituaries in serious newspapers that paid proper regard to the band's legacy and a glorious celebration of what he and his three colleagues had achieved.

This book is an unashamed celebration of the music of The Sweet and the lasting impact they have had on many bands that came afterwards.

Author's Note

All of The Sweet's studio albums from the 1970s are reviewed in full in the chapter for the year that they were originally released, along with summaries for the most significant compilation albums that were released during that period. Given that many of them did not originally appear on a studio album at the time, The Sweet's singles and associated B-sides are also reviewed in the relevant chapter for the year that they were released.

There were often very considerable differences between the band's UK and US catalogues throughout the 1970s. The detailed reviews, track listings and release information in each chapter relate to UK album and single releases. However, where relevant, information on US releases and any noteworthy distinctions are included in the relevant section.

Some recordings from band concerts during the decade were also subsequently released as live albums. However, where these are referred to, they are referenced in the relevant chapter for the year that the concert took place, rather than the year that the live album was originally released. In numerous cases, this was a number of years later.

The band is referred to as 'The Sweet' in the chapters up until 1974, in line with what appeared on the credits of the band's releases. When discussing the band's history from April 1974 onwards, however, when the definite article was dropped from the band's name on recorded releases, the book, as far as possible, refers to them simply as 'Sweet'.

Chapter One: Early Years

The Sweetshop (soon to be renamed The Sweet) were formed in 1968 with Brian Connolly on vocals, Mick Tucker on drums, Frank Torpey on guitar and Steve Priest on bass. All four musicians were based around the west London/Middlesex area. Although Connolly was born in Glasgow, he had moved to Harefield, Middlesex, with his foster family as a child and, like the other three musicians, had been involved in a succession of local bands. One of Connolly's early bands was Generation X (not to be confused with the punk band of the same name a decade later), with whom he recorded a handful of unreleased demos. One of these early recordings was an original composition called 'On The Spotlight', written by Connolly and band guitarist Chris Eldridge. The song would resurface several years later as the B-side to The Sweet's 'Alexander Graham Bell' and cheekily re-credited to Connolly-Tucker-Scott-Priest. However, the original has been uploaded to YouTube in recent years and it is possible to compare this very early demo with the later version by The Sweet.

By early 1968, both Connolly and Tucker had spent a couple of years working together in a soul revue outfit called Wainwright's Gentlemen. The band is not only notable for having future members of The Sweet within its ranks but also future Deep Purple singer Ian Gillan, albeit that Gillan departed not long after Tucker joined and several months before Connolly got involved. Towards the latter part of their time in Wainwright's Gentlemen, Tucker and Connolly were also joined by Torpey, who had previously played alongside the drummer in an earlier band. Fractious internal band politics saw all three depart Wainwright's Gentlemen in quick succession. First Torpey and then Tucker were unceremoniously sacked, after which an infuriated Connolly decided to quit of his own accord. Tucker: 'One day my telephone rang, and it was Brian. And he said, 'How you doing? I've been thinking, do you fancy joining a band?' I said, 'Well, I don't as it happens.' I said, 'I'm going to give it another three months with this band because we had a record deal nearly happening.' So, he said, 'Yeah, that's what I thought you'd say.' He said, 'They fired you last night.''

The three musicians, Connolly, Tucker and Torpey, thus decided to try to find a bass player and form their own band. Steve Priest was already known to them and was in The Army, another west London soul-influenced band who had been working a similar circuit to Wainwright's

Gentleman. Prior to joining The Army, Priest had been in a band called
The Countdowns who, through connections via their lead singer Malcolm
Sergeant, were called upon to do a number of sessions for the legendary
but highly troubled and ultimately murderous music producer, Joe Meek.
The band were mainly being used to record demos of songs that would
be given to other artists on Meek's roster and none of The Countdowns'
recordings would be given an official release until many years later.
However, Priest can be heard playing both bass and harmonica on
'You Stole My Heart Away' credited to Malcolm And The Countdowns,
which was finally released in 1997 as part of a compilation of previously
unreleased Meek recordings. A plodding and not particularly inspiring
track, it only really stands out for Priest's fairly impressive harmonica
playing. Around the same time, in the summer of 1966, Priest was also
called upon to provide backing vocals on a couple of recordings for
another producer, John Carter. Unlike the Meek recordings, these were
actually released that year. The first, 'We Love The Pirate Stations' was a
Beach Boys-esque pastiche intended as a protest song about the Wilson
Government's intention to close down the pirate stations. It failed to
chart. The second, recorded with the same team but this time credited
to The Ministry Of Sound, was an altogether more credible affair entitled
'White Collar Worker'. 'We did one appearance at Tiles of Oxford Street
for Radio Luxembourg,' recalled Priest. 'This was the only airplay it got!
It was quite a good song but did absolutely nothing. I was taught a good
lesson to learn – in disappointment – very early on.'

Towards the end of his stint with The Army, Priest had shared a bill with
old acquaintances Wainwright's Gentlemen, which led to a post-gig chat
with Connolly and Tucker. This was followed up by a phone call from
Connolly asking him if he would be interested in joining a new four-piece
band. Thus, in February 1968, Priest made his way to a rehearsal to join
Connolly, Tucker and Torpey. The outfit that was to become The Sweet
was born. Priest: 'We had a very good blend vocally. We didn't just sit
down and go, 'Alright, here's your part'; we all knew our own parts.'

As well as working up their own cover versions of well-known and
not so well-known songs, the four also devoted considerable time to
coming up with a suitable name, eventually alighting on The Sweetshop.
Priest: 'There were many bands around at this time that had silly names
like Marmalade, Strawberry Jam or Strawberry Alarm Clock, and so we
managed to come up with a silly name too. We thought that Sweet Shop
would do it.'

Although the band were still only semi-pro at this stage, they were able to secure the services of an agent, Starlite Artists, who had a number of name bands such as Marmalade and The Tremeloes on their books. The newly-christened Sweetshop would play their debut gig on 9 March 1968 at the Hemel Hempstead Pavilion, a venue where all four members had previously performed with other bands. Priest: 'Our material was very varied. Nothing really original. Jimi Hendrix, Cream, The Byrds. Mainly vocal-dominant stuff.'

For a band that were later to become notorious as much for their over-the-top visual appearance as for their music, Priest recalled the band's stage wear in those early days: 'I wore a kaftan with beads and no shoes. Frank wore jeans and looked like a builder. He didn't like the idea of stage clothes. Mick and Brian wore frilly shirts with chiffon scarves.'

Numerous gigs followed, including a stint acting as backing band to female vocal trio The Paper Dolls, who had enjoyed one-off hit around that time. In those early months, The Sweetshop also found themselves a manager in Paul Beuselinck. As Paul Nicholas, he would later go on to find fame himself as a stage musical and TV actor. At this point, however, his sights were firmly set on a pop career, which had included a recent spell in Screaming Lord Sutch's Savages. While he was waiting for his own hoped-for music career to take off, Beuselinck/Nicholas contented himself working in music management and publishing. The latter, through employment with Mellin Music Publishing, led to a fortuitous connection with one Phil Wainman.

Wainman himself had initially been focused on a career as a musician, too. As a drummer, he had worked the European cabaret circuit in the early 1960s with a band called The High Grades. Returning to the UK, he then got involved with a band called The Paramounts for a period. Today, they are most famous for being the outfit that would later evolve into Procol Harum. Wainman then released a couple of drum-themed singles as part of The Quotations, a group of session players who would back visiting American artists on stage. Neither single was a success and so, in addition to his session work, Wainman was beginning to turn his attention to writing, publishing and producing. He co-wrote 'Little Games', a hit for The Yardbirds in 1967 and, like Paul Nicholas, was also employed by Mellin Music. Nicholas urged Wainman to come and see this new band he was managing, The Sweetshop. Wainman was impressed enough to want to produce them and set about finding a suitable song for their debut single.

Single Release
'Slow Motion' (Watkins) b/w 'It's Lonely Out There' (Siegel / Jay)
Personnel:

Brian Connolly: lead vocals

Steve Priest: bass guitar, backing vocals

Frank Torpey: guitar

Mick Tucker: drums, backing vocals

Additional personnel:

Alan Benson: piano

Produced at: Central Sound Studios, London and Jackson's Studios, Rickmansworth, May-June 1968 by Phil Wainman

UK release date: July 1968

Highest chart UK position: Did not chart

After initially flirting with the idea of doing a Bee Gees cover, Wainman eventually settled on 'Slow Motion', a song from a relatively unknown songwriter called David Watkins, who was a pianist from Wolverhampton. The B-side 'It's Lonely Out There' was a song that Mellin Music Publishing owned the rights to. A third, unused, track – a cover of the Bee Gees' 'Down To Earth' was also recorded.

Wainman was able to secure a one-off release deal with the Fontana record label. Unfortunately, before the band could even release their debut single, there was one other hurdle to contend with. A casual acquaintance of Connolly and Tucker, Mark Wirtz, was also as evidently impressed with the name Sweetshop as they were and in June 1968 released his own single, 'Barefoot And Tiptoe', under the exact same name. Although the record sank without trace and little was heard from this other Sweetshop ever again, it did mean that Connolly, Priest, Torpey and Tucker would have to come up with an alternative name pretty rapidly. 'As we were almost ready to start playing real gigs, we settled with The Sweet,' recalled Priest. Torpey: 'Things went well; we shortened our name to Sweet (easy to cross out shop and initial the contracts). Robert Mellin's idea as our name had been hijacked by another group.'.

The band, therefore, became The Sweet and their very first single was released by Fontana on 19 July 1968. Very much of its time, 'Slow Motion' is a pleasant enough slice of late 1960s psychedelic pop. It was unlikely to set the world alight – and nor did it. However, as debut singles go, 'Slow Motion' was not a bad start at all. It was certainly a little more sophisticated than subsequent bubblegum-flavoured singles that the band released, whether of the flop variety or the early Chinn and Chapman hits. Moreover, rather than the dreaded session men who were to arrive further on down the line, The Sweet were playing on their own record with their own instruments, albeit with the augmentation of one session player, Alan Benson, who was brought in on piano. Allegedly, Torpey struggled with some of the guitar parts, which is one of the reasons why Benson's piano dominates the song's intro. Nonetheless, Connolly's vocals are strong and with the additional harmonies from Priest and Tucker, we begin to get a glimpse of the magic that the three would later be capable of.

The B-side 'It's Lonely Out There' is pretty much in that same psychedelic pop vein. The idea of having the B-side in any way musically similar to the A-side is a format that The Sweet would depart from dramatically in subsequent years when the differences between the chart-hungry A-side and the hard-rocking B-side would become more and more apparent. Priest was later very dismissive of 'It's Lonely Out There' in his autobiography, but it does, at least, feature some lovely wailing psychedelic guitar courtesy of Torpey and, unlike the A-side, it is the guitar rather than the piano that is the dominant instrument. Priest: 'The B-side was written by Mellin's son or nephew or something and the only way we were to have the A-side was to use this awful song, too. Frank couldn't or wouldn't sing, so we only had three-part harmonies that I used to try and arrange just for the sake of fattening up the sound.'

The single was a flop, albeit it did help to raise the band's profile. A review in the *NME* that August said the single 'wasn't as draggy as the title implies' and praised its 'catching, West Coast harmonic sound'. The Sweet also recorded their debut session for BBC Radio, performing both sides of the single and a third, self-composed song. While there would not be a follow-up single for over a year, there would still be regular visits to the recording studio. The band were being called upon by Mellin Music to demo tracks destined for other artists, some of those demos featuring all four members and some with just Connolly alone laying down a guide vocal to a backing track by other musicians. With echoes of the unsuccessful 'We Love The Pirates' single two years previously, Priest was also called upon to provide vocals on another one-off novelty single, 'We All Love Tiny Tim', which had been written by Wainman and released under the name Peter Pan & Wendy. It would meet with a similar lack of chart success.

Live gigging also stepped up in the latter part of 1968 and early 1969. One of the bands The Sweet found themselves sharing a bill with during those early months was the original 'Mark 1' line-up of Deep Purple. Although The Sweet would later come to look on enviously at the critical acclaim that Deep Purple were scooping up, while they were being dismissed with the bubblegum tag, the histories of the two bands are strangely interconnected. 'Mark 2' Deep Purple vocalist, Ian Gillan, was lead singer of Wainwright's Gentleman prior to Connolly joining. Roger Glover, who would go on to be Deep Purple's bass-player in their 'Mark 2' line-up, was also a close friend of Connolly's around this time and the two of them shared a flat together. When The Sweet found themselves in need of a new guitarist, following the departure of Torpey in July 1969, it was Deep Purple's original bass player, Nick Simper, who recommended a replacement.

When Torpey left, tiring of the quality of the venues and the lack of money coming in and not seeing any future for the band, Connolly initially turned to Gordon Farrimer, another old colleague from the Wainwright's Gentlemen days. However, Farrimer was not tempted. According to Tucker, Nick Simper, who lived in the same neck of the woods as The Sweet's drummer, recommended that they check out Mick Stewart. Like the original Sweet members, Stewart had been in a succession of local bands throughout his teenage years and ended up alongside Simper in Johnny Kidd's last ever Pirates line-up, prior to Kidd's tragic death in 1966. After some abortive attempts at a post-Kidd Pirates outfit, Stewart then concentrated on session work, backing a succession of visiting American artists on UK tours. After joining The Sweet, Stewart remained with them through the second half of 1969 and the first half of 1970, but it was not a line-up that particularly gelled and Stewart's first gig with the band was an unmitigated disaster. Priest: 'We didn't throw him out because we had a load of gigs coming up and had already signed the contracts. We did, however, rehearse a little more and eventually started sounding like a real group again.'

Single Release
'Lollipop Man' (Hammond / Hazlewood) b/w **'Time'** (Connolly / Priest / Stewart / Tucker)
Personnel:
Brian Connolly: lead vocals
Steve Priest: bass guitar, backing vocals
Mick Stewart: guitar
Mick Tucker: drums, backing vocals
Produced at: Abbey Road Studios, London, Summer 1969 by John Burgess

UK release date: September 1969
Highest chart places: Did not chart

As well as a change in line-up, the band also had a change in management around this period, too. Paul Nicholas had dropped out at this stage, but a new opportunity opened up when the band were booked to play a club in Bearstead, Kent, which was managed by a man named Roger Easterby, who also managed several bands. In the subsequent weeks, Easterby added The Sweet to his roster. With Nicholas off the scene, it did mean that opportunities to record further singles with Phil Wainman had been lost, at least for the time being. However, rather impressively, Easterby managed to secure a deal with George Martin's Associated Independent Recording to release records via EMI's Parlophone label. A session was booked for The Sweet at the famous Abbey Road Studios. The recording could in no way be regarded as iconic as the studio, sadly. While 'Slow Motion' can be viewed as a creditable debut release, the same could not be said of 'Lollipop Man'. A sickly, sub-novelty record, 'Lollipop Man' was released in September 1969, the first in a series of three flop singles on Parlophone. 'Whoever chose this bit of crap for us must have been screwing someone important because I could see no other reason for putting it on plastic,' Priest reflected. Connolly was even more scathing: ''Lollipop Man' was shit. Everything they gave us to record was shit.'

Record Mirror reviewed the single in September 1969, stating: 'The use of deep voice is pretty hammy, but the basic feel is commercial and direct and staccato.' Both the A-side and accompanying B-side were destined to remain largely unheard, though. Like its predecessor, this was to be another flop.

The B-side of 'Lollipop Man' was a band composition entitled 'Time'. The song is based around a fairly forgettable melody with a perfunctory guitar solo from new-boy Mick Stewart. While it was still some way off being one of the legendary B-sides that the band would soon be laying down, it nevertheless acts as a notable showcase for Tucker's prowess at the drum stool, alongside Connolly's unmistakable lead vocal and the band's burgeoning, three-part harmonies.

For the next two and a half years, across changes in management, line-up, songwriters and record labels, the type of bubblegum pop that 'Lollipop Man' represented would come to define what the Sweet were about in terms of recorded output, certainly as far as the A-sides went. It would still be a while before it brought them any measure of success, but for this and the half dozen singles that came after it, it was going to be bubblegum all the way.

So, what exactly is bubblegum? In their comprehensive 2001 overview, *Bubblegum is the Naked Truth,* Kim Cooper and David Smay looked at numerous ways the term had tended to be used in seeking to define bubblegum:

1. The classic bubblegum era from 1967-1972;
2. Disposable pop music;
3. Pop music contrived and marketed to appeal to pre-teens;
4. Pop music produced in an assembly-line process, driven by producers and using faceless singers;
5. Pop music with that intangible, upbeat 'bubblegum' sound.

That classic bubblegum era, of which early Sweet are very much a part, was a musical trend that began in the US. In stark contrast to the counter-culturalism and quest for deeper meanings that propelled the psychedelic-influenced bands of the late 1960s, bubblegum was all about happy lyrics and simple melodies. It was very much aimed at pre-teens and very young teens rather than their older brothers and sisters. As Lester Bangs once memorably wrote in *Rolling Stone* magazine: 'The basic bubblegum sound could be described as the basic sound of rock 'n' roll – minus the rage, fear, violence and anomie.' In the world of bubblegum, it was the producer, rather than the artist, who was king. Band names were often studio confections for varying groups of session players, and if a band did exist outside the studio, it was very often not the same musicians who were on the records that bore the band's name. Although the phenomenon began in the States, with outfits like the 1910 Fruitgum Company, Ohio Express and the animated band The Archies – who made the ultimate bubblegum hit 'Sugar Sugar' – releases would make the top ten on both sides of the Atlantic. Soon home-grown bubblegum acts began appearing in the UK, with figures like writer-producer Tony Macauley, and song-writers Roger Cook and Roger Greenaway racking up numerous bubblegum hits with groups of session players and singers. This is the world that The Sweet were entering. They were, at least, still playing on their own records at this stage.

While The Sweet were struggling to get a hit, a young guitarist from Wrexham, Andy Scott, was also pursuing musical ambitions and seeking that all-important breakthrough. Like his future bandmates in the south of

England, Scott had worked his way through a series of local bands around North Wales. Similarly, by 1966 he had found himself part of a seven-piece soul-influenced ensemble, The Silverstones, who he had joined as bass player. Not long afterwards, Scott made his first television appearance, performing with the band on a regional TV talent show that went out in the West and Wales area. This was followed by a series of appearances on the nationally networked *Opportunity Knocks*. A November 1966 article in a local newspaper *The Leader* enthusiastically noted that the band would be making their fourth appearance on the show in as many months and carried a message from the band's manager urging local people to cast a vote for The Silverstones. The band were much sought-after fixtures on the live circuit and in 1967 supported the Jimi Hendrix Experience in Manchester. It was a life-defining moment for Scott and vocalist Ted Yeadon, who were both keen to embrace a new direction. It was not a vision shared by the whole group, however. Line-up changes and a change in musical direction thus saw the group evolve into The Elastic Band. Scott recollects that the change in name was intended to reflect that the band 'could play a multitude of instruments and musically it had no boundaries.' The new set-up saw Scott playing lead guitar in addition to sharing bass duties with saxophone player, Tony Hannaby. The latter was soon replaced by Scott's own brother, Mike Scott, who also played bass and saxophone. The band released two heavily Mod-influenced singles on Decca, 'Think Of You Baby' and 'Do Unto Others', but another change in direction was beckoning and a venture into more jazzy, progressive territory. An album followed: *Expansions On Life*. When it was re-released in 2009, the review from *Record Collector* magazine noted:

> When they finally made it to the studio in 1969, their music was a long way from the highly-collectable mod pop of their two early singles, incorporating psych with an amateur proggishness, which remains very endearing, if not very well recorded. Step forward this reissue, which does right some of the studio wrongs and makes intrinsically good tracks such as 'Crabtree Farm' and 'Has Anybody Seen Her' sound as they should have done at the time. The addition of four bonus tracks and a wealth of archival material also goes some way to putting this very decent album back into some order.

It was certainly very different from the bubblegum pop direction that The Sweet were heading in and *Expansions On Life* is an enjoyable album of bluesy, psychedelic early prog that fans of the likes of Traffic, Syd Barrett-era Pink Floyd et al would appreciate. A second album was also recorded under the pseudonym of The Cool, but this was intended purely for a strictly limited release as a music library soundtrack album for film and TV use. There were a handful of TV appearances, including a prestigious slot on BBC2's *Colour Me Pop* programme. However, the band was hit by a bombshell before *Expansions On Life* was even released. Vocalist and multi-instrumentalist Ted Yeadon had decided to leave to pursue an offer to replace singer Steve Ellis in Love Affair. With commitments to fulfil, the band continued with Andy Scott and his brother Mike handling vocals. An opportunity to work as backing musicians for Liverpool-based poetry/comedy trio, The Scaffold, also arose and they carried out a number of live and studio engagements in this guise. However, relations began to sour and there was a feeling that the comedy trio were relying too much on The Elastic Band members for developing musical ideas, without the band receiving any credit. Nothing seemed to be quite working out as planned, and in late 1969 Andy Scott and his brother Mike made the decision to relocate to London.

Chapter Two: 1970 – The Classic Foursome Is Complete

1970 would be a very significant year for The Sweet. Although formed two years previously with a handful of flop singles behind them, the start of the new decade would see The Sweet team up with a new songwriting team, new management and an old familiar face as producer, whereupon they would enter the studio to lay down the vocals for what would eventually be their first hit single 'Funny Funny'. The year would also see The Sweet sign up to a new record label and audition for a new guitarist. Andy Scott would join the three existing members to complete the band's classic line-up towards the end of the year. Moreover, not only would 1970 be the year that things would start coming together for the band itself, it was also the year that things would start coming together professionally for three of the absolutely pivotal figures in the band's early successes, namely Nicky Chinn, Mike Chapman and Phil Wainman.

Single Release
'All You'll Ever Get From Me' (Cook / Greenaway) b/w 'The Juicer' (Stewart)
Personnel:
Brian Connolly: lead vocals
Steve Priest: bass guitar, backing vocals
Mick Stewart: guitar
Mick Tucker: drums, backing vocals
Produced at: Abbey Road Studios, London, 1969 by John Burgess and Roger Easterby
UK release date: January 1970
Highest chart places: Did not chart

The year began with the release of the single 'All You'll Ever Get From Me'. It was written by songwriting team Roger Cook and Roger Greenaway, who were responsible for a slew of chart hits in the late 1960s and early 1970s. A slice of light, inoffensive, bubblegum pop, it avoids the more cloying novelty aspects of the previous single. Indeed, the feel of 'All You'll Ever Get From Me' is not so far away from the sound of some of The Sweet's early Chinn-Chapman hits, the first of which would be recorded later that year. The B-side 'The Juicer' is credited to Mick Stewart alone, but Stewart later confirmed that it was actually a band composition, not that it made much difference to him one way or the other, given he claimed that he never received a penny in royalties. Authorship aside, if anything were to act as an early signal of intent as to how the band would utilise the medium of the single B-side to deliver powerful, uncompromising, high-octane hard rock, then this was it. Killer vocals from Connolly, Priest and Tucker coalesce with a hard-rocking rhythm section and some great guitar work from Stewart. It was an early foretaste of what, with a slight change in line-up, was to come.

The single picked up a lukewarm, unenthusiastic review in *Record Mirror,* although the band were also invited to do a Radio One session for the BBC in February, performing both sides of the single. Other publicity appearances and airplay followed yet, just as with 'Slow Motion' and 'Lollipop Man' before it, 'All You'll Ever Get From Me' once again failed to make the charts.

Single Release
'Get On The Line' (Barry / Kim) b/w 'Mr. McGallagher' (Stewart)

Personnel:
Brian Connolly: lead vocals
Steve Priest: bass guitar, backing vocals
Mick Stewart: guitar
Mick Tucker: drums, backing vocals
Additional personnel:
The Lady Birds: backing vocals
Clem Cattini: drums
Various session musicians
Lew Warburton: arranger, conductor.
Produced at: Abbey Road Studios, London, 1970 by John Burgess and Roger Easterby
UK release date: June 1970
Highest chart places: Did not chart

There was one final single for Parlophone. 'Get On The Line' was full-on bubblegum. A cover of a track that appeared on The Archies' 1969 album *Jingle Jangle* which was written by Andy Kim and Jeff Barry, the team behind 'Sugar Sugar', The Sweet were now fully ensconced in the world of the lightweight, the disposable and the saccharine. To add insult to injury, the band themselves were not even playing on this record, something they would have to get used to on a number of subsequent singles. Priest takes up the story in his autobiography (*Are You Ready Steve?*, 1994): 'Things start to get away from us after ('All You'll Ever Get From Me') and session men were brought in to do the next release called 'Get On The Line'. The only band member performing on the song was Brian. They wouldn't even let us sing background vocals. Instead, it was done, of all things, by The Lady Birds, who were a trio of women who would sing on shows like Benny Hill. This was very insulting to us.'

Again, as another foretaste of what was to follow, the band did at least get to play on the B-side. 'Mr McGallagher' was another band composition credited to Stewart. Although not as strong as the previous B-side 'The Juicer', it nevertheless helped to keep The Sweet's rock flip-side flame alive. A reasonably catchy, mid-paced rocker with a nice guitar break in the middle that was fairly typical for the period, it was infinitely preferable to the A-side but, once again, destined to be heard by very, very few.

However, one fortuitous encounter at the BBC studios in June 1970 led The Sweet to reconnect, once more, with Phil Wainman, the producer of the band's debut single two years previously. Visiting the BBC to record another Radio One session, Connolly and Tucker bumped into Wainman, who had recently begun working with a newly-formed songwriting duo, Mike Chapman and Nicky Chinn.

One half of the songwriting partnership, Australian-born Chapman, had been part of an outfit called Tangerine Peel. Reflecting back on the early days of his career, Chapman told authors John Tobler and Stuart Grundy for their book *The Record Producers* in 1983:

I played guitar and sang in those days (1967–69), and then I decided that my plans to be a rock'n'roll star were probably fruitless, so I decided to be a songwriter instead, which was a very wise decision, although I had wanted to be a rock star for something like sixteen years, and then in five minutes one day, I looked at myself in the mirror and told myself I'd be better locked away in a control room out of sight of the public. I'd been in a band called Tangerine Peel, and the music we were playing was really not the kind of music I liked. Basically, I liked commercial top forty hit music that I heard on the radio, while the group was playing more abstract stuff, psychedelic music. I think that one of the reasons for the group's failure was that when I started writing songs seriously, they were so simple and moronic that the rest of the band didn't want to play them, so I either had to perform my songs myself, which had no chance of success, or find a different outlet for them, which is why I gave up as a singer and performer.

Tangerine Peel's *Soft Delights* album was released by RCA Victor in 1970. Although the band had started out during the late 1960s psychedelic boom, by the time *Soft Delights* was released, more conventional pop influences were clearly apparent. As well as handling the vocals, eight of the ten songs on the album are credited to Chapman alone and he is co-writer of one more. A mixture of up-tempo pop and overwrought ballads, two songs, in particular, stand out. Opening track 'Cindy Lou' has a proto-glam 1950s jukebox vibe and would not have sounded at all out of place on, say, a Mud album a few years later. The title track, meanwhile, is such an archetypal slice of bubblegum pop that is so redolent of the type of material that they would soon be writing for The Sweet that, had Connolly's vocals replaced Chapman's, you would have sworn blind it was a long-lost Sweet number.

Nicky Chinn, meanwhile, was the son of a wealthy businessman who ran a string of service stations and car dealerships. Chinn was also looking to pursue a career in music and had already made modest inroads as a songwriter prior to meeting Chapman. He had been recruited by a friend, former Manfred Mann vocalist Mike D'Abo, to assist with lyrics on a couple of numbers for the soundtrack of the 1970 film *There's A Girl In My Soup* which starred Peter Sellers. Chinn met Chapman while the latter was a waiter at Tramp, a West End nightclub that Chinn frequented. The two decided to team up. Chinn (in *The Record Producers* again):

> I think every kid wants to be a rock star at some stage. But unlike Mike, for example, it never got beyond standing in front of a mirror pretending I was playing a guitar when I was just in my teens or pretending to mime to a record. But I never had any serious aspirations to rock stardom because I simply cannot sing, so although I had the very normal early teenage fantasies, it was never part of my realistic goals.

Wainman had already been introduced to Chinn as a potential songwriter for his burgeoning recording operation, but it was only when Chapman came on the scene that things began to take shape. While Wainman was unimpressed by the new duo's first couple of attempts, a conversation ensued about the success of The Archies' 'Sugar Sugar' the previous year. Chinn and Chapman were thus primed to come up with something similar and returned to Wainman with a song called 'Funny Funny'. Chapman (again in *The Record Producers*):

> 'Funny Funny' was the first result of my personal musical preferences in the late sixties and early seventies, which were for bubblegum music, and in particular for a record called 'Sugar Sugar' by the Archies, which is still, to this day, one of my favourite records of all time. Basically, 'Funny Funny' started off as a poor rip-off of 'Sugar Sugar', which is not to say that I thought it was a bad song. But compared with what we went on to create – the more imaginative stuff – I think it was a little tedious, but I think if I put that record on now, I'd be pretty happy with the way it sounded.

Wainman booked a session at Recorded Sound Studios in London to put together a demo that they could hawk around potential record labels. Chapman sang vocals, with Wainman on drums and with session players Pip Williams on guitar, John Roberts on bass and Fiachra Trench on keyboards. Things moved on rapidly from there. It was around this time that Wainman bumped into The Sweet on that fateful day at the BBC studios. In response to a request from Tucker about whether he had any decent songs to offer them, Wainman arranged a meeting where he played them the 'Funny Funny' demo. They were evidently impressed. Within a short space of time, not only did they agree to put their own vocals on the demo, they also agreed to abandon Roger Easterby, unravel themselves from their existing recording contract and allow Chinn and Chapman to manage them. Wainman: 'I'd only just been introduced to Chinn and Chapman and I did have 'Funny Funny' and I said it would be great if you put your voices on 'Funny Funny' … They turned up and they did the vocals, and the vocals were great, and they actually did it credit. They really did.'

Getting the band signed up to a new record company, however, proved more difficult and, initially, Wainman, Chinn and Chapman struggled to find a label to release 'Funny Funny'. Indeed, while the two songwriters were able to successfully place another of their songs ('Tom Tom Turnaround') with Mickie Most's RAK label for release by the Australian pop outfit New World, they failed to elicit any enthusiasm for 'Funny Funny'. Chinn and Chapman eventually hooked up with Philips and a contract was about to be signed when they were suddenly informed that key figures from the management team would be leaving Philips and decamping en masse to RCA. Even though RCA was one of the labels that had previously rejected 'Funny Funny' they were assured that the new team would make the single a priority and a contract with RCA was duly signed.

While it was to mark a major turn in fortunes for The Sweet, Priest was to reflect on the situation very differently in later years: 'What a stupid thing for us to allow them to do. We were being controlled by a couple of novices. Mike Chapman could write what sounded like hit songs, but Nicky was brought up in a private boys' school and didn't know his arse from his elbow.'

In the summer of 1970, Mick Stewart, feeling similar frustrations that Frank Torpey had experienced the previous year, decided to leave the band. On learning that a new recording deal was in the offing, Stewart subsequently had a change of heart – but it was too late. Wainman knew Stewart already and had made it clear to the remaining three that he had no interest in working with him. The band would have to find themselves a new guitarist. An advert was placed in *Melody Maker* and auditions held in London's Shepherd's Bush. 'To our great surprise there was a line of players all around the block,' recalled Priest. Andy Scott was one of them. Chinn (interview: *Glitz, Blitz & Hitz*, 2003): 'Then Andy came and there was no question that he was the guy, and he was the final piece of the jigsaw.'

After relocating to London, Scott had initially tried his luck in a six-piece band called Mayfield's Mule. There, he teamed up with former Elastic Band drummer Sean Jenkins, and his own brother, Mike. Mayfield's Mule had scored a minor success with a single in 1969 prior to Scott joining. Scott, himself, went on to record a couple of singles with them, initially attracted by the notion of a twin lead guitar set-up, something that Wishbone Ash would go on to have great success with. The first Mayfield's Mule single to feature Scott was the countryish 'I See A River' followed by the soulful 'We Go Rollin' with its very Vanilla Fudge-like B-side 'My Way Of Living'. Neither single charted. Once again, it looked like another dead end for Scott: 'The band was too into the wrong kind of things, the dope counted more than the music and I couldn't handle that.' He thus enthused about a likely change of direction that The Sweet would bring him. As he told *Sounds* magazine in 1976:

I'd been with so many heavy-type bands I just went looking for refreshment, and I met Sweet. I'd heard a couple of their earlier records and I thought, I don't know if my head will let me handle this. Just from the record angle. But when I got to rehearsal, Brian wasn't there, only Stevie and me, and we just started blowing and I realised straight away that you shouldn't take things at their face value. I was no better a player than Mick and Steve and vice versa, we all had something going for us; we all seemed to fit. It was like a breath of fresh air for all of us. We were all into the same kind of music, and I played them a couple of things I'd written and they just sort of fell into it straight away, which was great.

With a new guitarist to quickly integrate into the band, and there having been no live gigs for several months as a result of all the recent changes, the band's new management arranged for the four to spend time rehearsing at a farmhouse in Wales. Scott made his official live debut with The Sweet at Redcar's Windsor Ballroom on 26 September 1970. 'When I joined, they were doing a lot of what I consider to be 'cheap covers'. They had the odd song that was really good, but all the obvious covers, like 'Paranoid' and Deep Purple things.' (*Blockbuster: The True Story of The Sweet*, Dave Thompson, 2010)

Scott soon made his presence felt, introducing some of his own songs to the set, alongside the covers and the handful of band originals from before Scott's time. The band also worked up a Who medley and a Motown set. Scott: 'The vocal thing came together as well because they were perfect with their ranges and then I had the voice.'

There would be more gigs around the UK during October, November and December 1970, including a corporate gig at the Royal Albert Hall for British Airways, as well a couple of sessions for BBC Radio. 'Funny Funny', meanwhile, recorded earlier in the year and overdubbed with vocals from Connolly, Priest and Tucker, would still not get a release until early in the New Year. However, at the tail-end of 1970, The Sweet did make their very first television appearance. Just before Christmas the band visited Granada TV studios where they performed 'Funny Funny' for the *Lift Off* show which was broadcast on 30 December. Seemingly, things were finally beginning to fall into place for The Sweet.

Chapter Three: 1971 – First Hits

1971 was the year that glam rock truly began taking off in the UK. T. Rex, evolving from a hippy acoustic duo to glammed-up pop icons, had released 'Ride A White Swan' in Autumn 1970, where it made its way up the charts to no. 2 in January 1971, to be followed by 'Hot Love', 'Get It On' and 'Jeepster' that same year. After several years of gigging and numerous flop singles, Slade also hit their stride in 1971, with the raucous 'Get Down And Get With It' becoming their first hit, followed by 'Coz I Luv You' and 'Look Wot You Dun'. 1971 would be the year that The Sweet had their first hits, too. However, The Sweet's competitors sound-wise at this stage, were not the likes of T. Rex and Slade, or anyone else in the evolving glam rock scene for that matter. Rather, The Sweet would be firmly placed in the bubblegum camp, purveyors of impossibly upbeat, saccharine, lightweight and disposable pop – competing with the likes of Middle Of The Road's 'Chirpy Chirpy Cheep Cheep' and Dawn's 'Knock Three Times'.

Single Release
'Funny Funny' (Chapman / Chinn) b/w **'You're Not Wrong For Loving Me'** (Connolly / Priest / Scott / Tucker)
Personnel:
Brian Connolly: lead vocals
Steve Priest: bass guitar, backing vocals
Andy Scott: guitar, backing vocals
Mick Tucker: drums, backing vocals
Additional personnel:
John Roberts: bass
Phil Wainman: drums, percussion
Pip Williams: guitar
Fiachra Trench: keyboards
Produced at Recorded Sound Studios and Nova Sound Studios, London, June-July 1970 and September 1970 by Phil Wainman
UK release date: January 1971
Highest chart places: UK: 13, Germany: 5, US: Did not chart

'Funny Funny' was finally released in January 1971. Sales were slow at first. The compilation of statistics from record shops was hit by a postal strike, which made it difficult for new entrants aiming for the top 40. By

March, however, 'Funny Funny' at last entered the charts. Tony Blackburn made it 'Record of the Week' for his Radio One show. Airplay and media exposure steadily grew. Peaking at no. 13 in May 1971, The Sweet finally had their first hit. Not only was it a hit in the UK, but the record sold substantially in mainland Europe and South Africa, too. While its trite lyrics and simple melody borrowed heavily from The Archies, and while none of the band were playing on the record and only three of them were actually singing on it, it was, nevertheless, a hit. It would seem that the release had a somewhat devious helping hand to ensure it broke the charts, not uncommon at the time. Steve Priest: 'He (Chinn) sent Phil and Mike around the country to all the stores whose sales were used to compile the Top 30. Between them, they purchased vast quantities of our new release, brought them back to London and dumped them in the Thames.' No matter, The Sweet had finally achieved what had hitherto eluded them – a hit single.

Scott: 'I remember my brother looking at me and going, 'Are you sure? You've been in a band that's been more akin to Jethro Tull and you're going into a band that's going to have a three-chord wonder. I can see why,' he said. 'It stinks of being a hit.' But he said, in his eyes, 'Are you selling out?'. I said, wait until you hear the B-sides.'

The B-side of The Sweet's first hit was 'You're Not Wrong For Loving Me'. Although the song was credited as a band composition, it was actually written by Scott alone during his Elastic Band days but suggested to Phil Wainman as a possible B-side to 'Funny Funny'. A mellow acoustic track built around the band's love of vocal harmony groups like the Beach Boys and Three Dog Night, it showed a degree of musical maturity that was absent on the A-side. Nevertheless, it was a long way away from many of the harder-edged recordings that the band would soon be offering up as B-sides. Scott took the view that putting forward an acoustic track for their first RCA B-side would be the easiest way for the band to get Wainman on side and ensure that those all-important songwriting royalties came through to them, at the same time as demonstrating what the band were capable of musically. 'If we'd have come with 'Done Me Wrong Alright' then and there he'd probably have rejected it,' reflected Scott.

The band's live schedule had ramped up considerably since Scott first joined them. As well as occasional TV appearances and BBC radio sessions The Sweet were now extensively gigging around the UK. In the previous year, with the band being without a guitarist for some months and with changes in both management and record labels, it meant that

The Sweet only ended up performing around a dozen concerts. During the course of 1971, however, The Sweet would clock up around 130 live dates. Moreover, chart success meant that the small nondescript clubs began giving way to larger ballrooms and occasional European jaunts. The band's media profile, too, began cranking up at this stage. In March 1971 Mickie Most's brother, David Most, was appointed as the band's publicist. From now on there would be frequent appearances in the music press and a succession of interviews with band members, alongside reviews for each single.

Such interviews were not always exactly helpful to the band, however, as they dodged around the contradictory demands of being bubblegum pop stars singing along to someone else's tunes and the desire for creative recognition for their own musical output. 'We won't get labelled because we're progressing with new and different singles,' Connolly rather optimistically told one interviewer. 'We want to prove to people that we're versatile and not a bubblegum group.'

Single Release
'Co-Co' (Chapman / Chinn) b/w 'Done Me Wrong All Right' (Connolly / Priest / Scott / Tucker)

Personnel:
Brian Connolly: lead vocals
Steve Priest: bass guitar, backing vocals
Andy Scott: guitar, backing vocals
Mick Tucker: drums, backing vocals
Additional personnel:
John Roberts: bass
Phil Wainman: drums, percussion
Pip Williams: guitar
Produced at Island Studios, London and Central Sound Studios, London, March-April 1971 by Phil Wainman
UK release date: June 1971
Highest chart places: UK: 2, Germany: 1, US: 99

The band's second single via Chinn and Chapman, 'Co-Co', was released on 21 May 1971. In a conversation about potential future songwriting ideas that Chinn and Chapman might turn their attention towards, Wainman had sung the praises of the calypso-style song 'Montego Bay'. This had been a one-off hit for Blobby Bloom the previous year. It clearly succeeded in planting the germ of an idea in Chapman's head. Wainman: 'Mike Chapman turned up and said, 'What do you think of this for The Sweet?' He said we could use steel drums and everything.'

A simple melody with an infectious rhythm built around bass guitar and piano with steel drums and a breezily tropical Caribbean feel, 'Co-Co' was ideally placed to be a summer smash. Reviewing it for the *NME*, Derek Johnson declared it an 'obvious hit' and raved about its 'captivating Latin flavour and a mellow steel drum sound', arguing there was 'more substance and sheer guts' to it than their previous single. While he was perhaps right in detecting a slightly more sophisticated stab at writing a song, even the most devoted fans of 'Co-Co' would be unlikely to commend it on account of its substance and guts. However, as one of those silly but utterly infectious songs that become a ubiquitous summer hit, the Caribbean-flavoured rhythms and simple melody ensured its success, where it would be joined over the years by the likes of 'Y Viva Espana', 'The Birdie Song' and 'Agadoo'. 'Co-Co' climbed to no. 2 in the UK charts and was a hit across much of Europe, second only to the even more ubiquitous and even sillier 'Chirpy Chirpy Cheep Cheep'.

While the likes of Slade and T. Rex may have had more commercial-sounding songs on the A-sides of their singles, their B sides were not necessarily a radical departure in terms of overall sound. The flip-side to 'Co-Co' could not have been more different to the A-side, however. While the B-side to 'Funny Funny' was a light, introspective acoustic-driven number, 'Done Me Wrong All Right' is a hard-rocking blues song that really begins to unleash some of the classic Sweet sounds that we would soon become familiar with. The song cannot be described in any way as glam rock but with lyrics invoking traditional 1950s rock and roll imagery ('shades of Jerry Lee') and those perennial rock and roll themes of debauchery and wronged lovers (as opposed to coyly sweet bubblegum themes) the song appears to pre-empt the sound of the future Sweet with far more accuracy than the A-side could ever hope to.

'Done Me Wrong All Right' was certainly a world away from what Chinn and Chapman were writing at the time. 'In the early period, we needed each other,' recalled Tucker in a 1976 interview, 'But when we started to get more into writing our own material, the relationship with them became detrimental to us. We were brainwashed into believing we were totally dependent on Mike and Nicky. They never took any interest in our own writing; they were only interested in their A-sides, their own songs. The A-sides and B-sides, which we wrote ourselves, sounded like two different bands.'

Nevertheless, from these early days, the band had an awareness that writing their own material, albeit only for the B-sides, would be extremely important to them, not just creatively but financially, too. The four members had decided at the start that, regardless of who was first to come up with an initial idea for a particular song, all four members would work to develop it, and each would receive a songwriting credit. To consolidate their writing income further, the band formed their own publishing company Sweet Publishing Ltd. which was incorporated in June 1971 and ensured publishing income flowed directly to the band members rather than being split with their management/production team.

In the summer of 1971, The Sweet embarked on a UK tour with additional jaunts to continental Europe, including a number of dates in Sweden. As an indication of just how 'managed' the band were at this stage, Priest complained in his autobiography that not only was the band's set-list chosen for them but so, too, was their stage clothing. A feel for the band's stage act at that time can be gleaned from listening to a live concert they performed for the Swedish Broadcasting Corporation on 13 September 1971. Since the 1990s, this has been available on CD. As well as slightly punchier versions of 'Funny Funny', 'Co-Co' and other Chinn-Chapman pop offerings, a harder-edged side of The Sweet is also on display as the band race their way through a medley of Eddie Cochran, Little Richard and Gary U.S. Bonds hits and conclude their set with a blast of Jerry Lee Lewis's 'Great Balls Of Fire'.

There were also more sessions for the BBC. Although The Sweet had recorded a handful of sessions prior to that, by 1971, they were frequent visitors to the BBC's Maida Vale studios. While a number of these sessions included the early hit singles, the band also had a chance to unleash their rock 'n' roll energy with tracks like their own 'Done Me Wrong All Right' and some muscular covers of songs from the likes of Eddie Cochran and Little Richard. These 1971 sessions also reveal something of a Who obsession, too, as the band deliver their take on a number of Townshend classics. While the song choices of Who covers and 1950s rock 'n' roll are not perhaps the most imaginative ever, they nevertheless provide demonstrable proof at this early stage that this is a band that can deliver riff-heavy hard rock with gorgeous soaring vocal harmonies. Although the sound quality on some recordings is patchy, highlights from many of these sessions were given an official release for the very first time on the *Sweet*

At The Beeb disc, which was released by Sony as part of the 2017 Sweet box set.

Single Release
'Alexander Graham Bell' (Chapman / Chinn) b/w **'Spotlight'** (Connolly / Priest / Scott / Tucker)
Personnel:
Brian Connolly: lead vocals
Steve Priest: bass guitar, backing vocals
Andy Scott: guitar, backing vocals
Mick Tucker: drums, backing vocals
Additional personnel:
John Roberts: bass
Phil Wainman: drums, percussion
Pip Williams: guitar
Fiachra Trench: arrangements
Produced at Nova Sound Studios and Central Sound Studios, London, Summer 1971 by Phil Wainman
UK release date: October 1971
Highest chart places: UK: 33, Germany: 24, US: Not released

Released in October 1971, 'Alexander Graham Bell', the band's next single for RCA, was something of a departure in comparison to the bubblegum choruses and cheesy hooks of the previous two singles. A slower-paced song with brass accompaniment about the inventor of the telephone it seems a curious lyrical theme for a band making bubblegum records. However, Australian band The Mixtures had released something similar earlier that year with their single 'Henry Ford'. In his autobiography, Priest blasts 'Alexander Graham Bell' as a 'terrible song' and a 'direct rip-off'. Perhaps Chinn and Chapman should have taken note of the 'Henry Ford' record's failure, however. Compared to The Mixture's 'Pushbike Song' which made no. 1 in Australia and no. 2 in Britain, their paean to Henry Ford struggled to scrape into the charts at all. A similar fate was to befall The Sweet. Despite relatively favourable reviews in *NME* and *Record Mirror,* the release failed to make much of an impact on the UK charts, climbing to just no. 33 after the huge success of 'Co-Co' in the summer.

'Spotlight', a song that Connolly had a hand in writing in his pre-Sweet days, was repurposed as the hard-rocking flip-side and credited to Connolly-Priest-Scott-Tucker. Combining a great lead vocal from Connolly and those beautiful harmonies from the rest of the boys, alongside searing lead guitar from Scott, it shows the band really hitting their stride with their B-sides at this stage.

Album Release
Gimme Dat Ding – The Sweet (Side 1) and The Pipkins (Side 2)

Personnel (Side 1 only):

Brian Connolly: lead vocals

Steve Priest: bass guitar, backing vocals

Mick Stewart: guitars

Mick Tucker: drums, backing vocals

Additional personnel:

Lew Warburton: arranger, conductor (track 5)

Tracks 1 and 2 produced at Abbey Road Studios, London, 1969, by John Burgess; tracks 3-6 produced at Abbey Road Studios, London, 1969-70 by John Burgess and Roger Easterby

UK release date: October 1971

Highest chart places: Did not chart

Running time (Side 1 only): 16:45

Track listing (Side 1): 1. Lollipop Man (Hammond / Hazlewood) 2. Time (Connolly / Priest / Stewart / Tucker) 3. All You'll Ever Get from Me (Cook / Greenaway) 4. The Juicer (Stewart) 5. Get On The Line (Barry / Kim) 6. Mr. McGallagher (Stewart)

The band's first studio album was scheduled for release the month after 'Alexander Graham Bell' came out. First, however, EMI were to sneak in with a rush-released compilation on their budget Music For Pleasure label. Parlophone had already tried their luck with a re-release of the 'All You'll Ever Get From Me' single, but it failed to chart. Side one of the compilation features the band's three flop Parlophone singles (although not the band's debut single which was released on the Fontana label) along with their respective B-sides. Obviously, this meant there was not enough material to fill a whole album, so EMI's solution was to devote side two to the Tony Burrows / Roger Greenaway novelty act, The Pipkins, who had enjoyed a hit with 'Gimme Dat Ding' the previous year. Even for the time, such a hybrid mish-mash was weird, but, nevertheless, the *Gimme Dat Ding* compilation was to be the first album release to bear the Sweet name.

Original pressings of the album bear a copyright date of 1970, but the album itself was not released until 1971. It was a cash-in on the back of the success of the two recent RCA singles, as the album sleeve-notes make clear: 'The Sweet are a foursome who stormed the charts in March 1971 with their recording of 'Funny Funny' and followed it up with an even bigger success, 'Co-Co.'

Moreover, the blatant cash-in extends to the front cover artwork, which bears a photo of The Sweet with new-boy Andy Scott, alongside a second photo of The Pipkins in their novelty costumes. Scott, of course, was not even in the band when these singles were recorded, and it was Mick Stewart who was the band's guitarist at the time. Despite EMI's efforts in repackaging the band's early singles to try and grab some of the success that had come the band's way since switching to RCA, the album failed to chart. As Tucker later reflected, 'What pissed us off, apart from the album being such crap, was that EMI put far more effort into us after we'd left them than they ever did while we were with the label.'

Later attempts at repackaging the early pre-hit singles, such as *The Sweet – First Recordings 1968-1971,* would thankfully eschew padding out the early releases with The Pipkins but would instead include additional unreleased tracks, some of which were not Sweet recordings at all but were simply Connolly laying down a guide vocal to another band's demo. At least it was Connolly on these and not The Pipkins, though!

Album Release
Funny How Sweet Co-Co Can Be

Personnel:

Brian Connolly: lead vocals (except track 2)

Steve Priest: bass guitar, backing vocals, lead vocals (track 2)

Andy Scott: guitars, backing vocals

Mick Tucker: drums, backing vocals

Additional personnel:

John Roberts: bass

Phil Wainman: drums, percussion

Pip Williams: guitar, arrangement

Fiachra Trench: arrangements

Produced at Nova Sound Studios, London, 1971 by Phil Wainman

UK release date: November 1971

Highest chart places: UK: Did not chart, Germany: Did not chart, US: Not released

Running time: 37:14

In the wake of *Gimme Dat Ding*, The Sweet's first studio album proper was *Funny How Sweet Co-Co Can Be* which was released in November 1971. A curious mixture of bubblegum, cabaret and hard rock, the album brought together the first two RCA singles, a handful of other Chinn-Chapman songs, three band compositions and a couple of covers. 'As usual, we weren't allowed to play on most of it and really had little to do with the choice of material,' Priest subsequently noted.

It is worth taking a moment to consider the overall lyrical themes on this debut studio album, particularly when compared to later albums the band would go on to record over the course of the decade. Little boys dancing in the Caribbean, native Americans and woodchop men are archetypal bubblegum fodder that dominate the album, along with the more traditional pop themes of love and heartache. With the exception of 'Done Me Wrong All Right', which was only added on later versions of the album, there is certainly little in the way of those traditional rock and roll staples: sex and fast cars and the rock 'n' roll lifestyle. 'We do present a smart, clean and colourful image,' Connolly said in one interview at the time. 'I suppose you could say we're a long-haired version of a lot of short-haired pop groups.' That outlook would change dramatically with later releases, of course.

The album appeared in two completely different covers when it was originally released, both about as subtle as the words to the average bubblegum hit. The first, for the UK market, featured the band in a posed group shot superimposed in the middle of a boiled sweet wrapper on a beige hessian background. The second, for the German release, featured a black and white live shot of the band on stage, with a big cartoon pot of golden honey being poured all over them.

'Co-Co' (Chapman / Chinn)
Leaving off the recently released 'Alexander Graham Bell' altogether, the album opens with the band's no. 2 smash from earlier that year – not that they are playing on it, of course, only singing.

'Chop Chop' (Chapman / Chinn)
Aside from the two hits 'Funny Funny' and 'Co-Co', the other Chinn-Chapman material on the album is a mixed bag that seemed to consist of whatever the two writers happened to have lying around, including a couple of songs that had been hits for other acts. The first of these was 'Chop Chop' which had been released as a single by Radio One DJ, Tony

Blackburn. On this Sweet version, the lead vocals are handled by Priest.
A piece of bubblegum silliness in the style of 'Funny Funny' and 'Co-Co',
though nowhere near as catchy, the dominant instruments are Fiachra
Trench's organ and piano.

'Reflections' (Holland / Dozier / Holland)

It is with the two covers that the album really veers off into hackneyed
cabaret renditions. The first of these is 'Reflections', a hit for Diana Ross
& The Supremes in 1967. While its psychedelic vibe was seen as quite a
ground-breaking development for The Supremes back then, The Sweet's
cover comes across as a fairly anodyne Motown pastiche, albeit that it at
least provides a showcase for Connolly's distinctive vocal.

'Honeysuckle Love' (Connolly / Priest / Scott / Tucker)

On the original UK release, only three band compositions appeared on
the album (although a fourth was added on the version aimed at the
mainland European market). While the remainder of these compositions
would also serve as single B-sides, the one band composition that did
not also turn up as a B-side is 'Honeysuckle Love'. Brought to the band
by Scott, it comes across as rather like The Sweet's own attempt to rival
Chinn and Chapman in the bubblegum stakes.

'Santa Monica Sunshine' (Chapman / Chinn)

One of the two Chinn-Chapman compositions on the album that had
neither been a single for The Sweet nor a single for another artist, 'Santa
Monica Sunshine' is a driving song with a bit of a country and western
feel. The lyrics are less inane than the more obvious bubblegum hits and
it is very reflective of the kind of lightweight, inoffensive pop that was
around at the dawn of the 1970s.

'Daydream' (Sebastian)

After the 'Reflections' cover earlier on, the band (or at least Wainman's
bunch of session players) then go on to murder John Sebastian's
'Daydream', a hit for the Lovin' Spoonful in 1966. The dreadful plinky-
plonk keyboards would have been familiar to anyone showing up at a
Butlins holiday camp ballroom or a third-rate variety night spectacular at
their local social club during that period and are a particular low point
on the album. By way of comparison, just compare The Sweet's appalling
rendition of 'Daydream' with Slade's powerful, soulful, imaginative cover

of another Lovin' Spoonful hit, namely 'Darlin' Be Home Soon' on the *Slade Alive* album around that same period.

'Funny Funny' (Chapman / Chinn)
The band's breakthrough hit from earlier in the year begins side two of the original vinyl album.

'Tom Tom Turnaround' (Chapman / Chinn)
Like 'Chop Chop' on the original side one, 'Tom Tom Turnaround' was the other Chinn-Chapman song that had been released by another artist. It had been a top ten hit for New World that summer. A maudlin slice of folk-pop, Connolly's lead vocal and the band's harmonies at least make it infinitely preferable to the New World original. Ostensibly a love song about two native Americans, it epitomised the banal, child-like story-telling approach, which was a regular lyrical device for Chinn and Chapman at that stage. Native Americans were to become something of a lyrical obsession for Chinn and Chapman in those first couple of years. Indeed, 'Red Indians' were a common preoccupation of bubblegum lyricists on the other side of the Atlantic, too, with songs like 'Indian Giver' being a hit for the 1910 Fruitgum Company in 1969.

'Jeanie' (Connolly / Priest / Scott / Tucker)
One of the stand-out tracks on the album, 'Jeanie' was also to reappear the following year as the B-side to 'Poppa Joe'. A bouncy, acoustic number with a slight Americana lilt, it is credited as a group composition but was actually brought to the band by Connolly. This was not without controversy, however, as the song's actual author was said to be Deep Purple's Roger Glover and a settlement had to be negotiated.

'Sunny Sleeps Late' (Chapman / Chinn)
The only other Chinn and Chapman number on the album that had not previously appeared as a single, either for The Sweet or another artist, 'Sunny Sleeps Late' is more lightweight early 1970s pop, this time with a really irritating pitter-patter percussion.

'Spotlight' (Connolly / Priest / Scott / Tucker)
Given that 'Done Me Wrong All Right' was missed off the UK release, the magnificent 'Spotlight', which had appeared as the B-side to 'Alexander Graham Bell' the previous month, was the only real hard rock moment

on the original album. As such, it remains the highlight of the album and the only track that can more than hold its own against material that would appear on the later Sweet albums that would have rock rather than bubblegum and cabaret at their core. Although credited to the band, the song originated in pre-Sweet days and began life as 'On The Spotlight', a song Connolly had written with guitarist Chris Eldridge, in one of his early bands. Uploaded to YouTube, it is possible to hear the original and compare the two.

'Done Me Wrong All Right' (Connolly / Priest / Scott / Tucker)

Curiously, the brilliant 'Done Me Wrong All Right', which had been the B-side to 'Co-Co' was missed off the original UK release. This is in spite of the track appearing on the German version of the album that was released, with a different cover and a slightly modified title, that same year. Perhaps 'Done Me Wrong All Right' ventured just that bit too far into hard rock territory for what Chinn and Chapman had in mind. As Priest would later say, 'It was Nicky Chinn's version of what he thought our album should be.'

Although the album picked up fairly positive reviews in the likes of *NME* and *Record Mirror* and sold reasonably well in the UK, it failed to make the charts, albeit reaching the top 20 in Denmark and no. 1 in Finland. Looking back, *Funny How Sweet...* has its moments but affords little opportunity for the band to showcase their obvious songwriting potential. Overall it is really a very lightweight and patchy affair, particularly when contrasted to the mesmerising impact of T. Rex's *Electric Warrior* (released in September 1971) or *Slade Alive* (released a few months later). The Sweet would get their moment in the sun when it came to releasing classic albums, of course, but they would have to wait several years for now.

Outside of the studio, The Sweet undertook a twenty-date tour of Germany during October and November 1971, with a handful of additional dates in the UK and Ireland. Prior to that, in late September, there was a slightly odd foray into the world of cabaret. The band had been signed up with an old-school booking agent, the Harold Davidson Agency, who, as well as securing dates at the usual clubs and theatres, booked the band in for a seven-night residency at the Excelsior Ballroom in Middlesbrough. 'We lasted three days and they paid us not to play,' recalled Scott. 'They paid us in full not to play. Thank God.'

The Sweet wound up the year in which they enjoyed their first taste of chart success with a New Year's Eve gig on Hastings Pier. They may have left the world of cabaret behind, but there would still be a few more months of bubblegum hits and session musicians to contend with before the band really began to develop a sound of their own sound and make their mark with that colourful and exciting new musical trend: glam rock.

Chapter Four: The Sweet Go Glam

The Sweet may have been behind the curve when glam rock took off in the previous year, but 1972 would be the year that they unequivocally and rather gloriously embraced this exciting new genre. Looking back at their first *Top Of The Pops* appearance of 1972 (in the February of that year where they performed 'Poppa Joe') it is not difficult to detect some of the visual impact of glam and glitter already, in terms of the band's sartorial style. However, the sounds they are miming along to are still a million miles away from anything approaching glam rock. Contrast that to the band's final appearance on *Top Of The Pops* that year (promoting 'Wig-Wam Bam') and the change that has taken place is very, very evident. Not only is Connolly's face festooned in glitter, silver trousers everywhere you look and Priest resplendent in full-length native American head-dress, but the band's sound, too has undergone a dramatic transformation. 1972 would be the year the Sweet go glam. First, however, there would be one more pure bubblegum single and one that ended up having a foot in both camps.

Single Release
'Poppa Joe' (Chapman / Chinn) b/w **'Jeanie'** (Connolly / Priest / Scott / Tucker)

Personnel:
Brian Connolly: lead vocals
Steve Priest: bass guitar, backing vocals
Andy Scott: guitar, backing vocals
Mick Tucker: drums, backing vocals
Additional personnel:
John Roberts: bass
Phil Wainman: drums, percussion
Pip Williams: guitar
Fiachra Trench: arrangements
Produced at Island Studios, London, and Central Sound Studios, London, November 1971 by Phil Wainman
UK release date: February 1972
Highest chart places: UK: 11, Germany: 3, US: Did not chart

After the relative failure of 'Alexander Graham Bell' Chinn and Chapman returned to the formula that they had so successfully deployed on 'Co-

Co': maddeningly infectious choruses, cod calypso rhythms and lots of steel drums. Released in February 1972, 'Poppa Joe' 'reverted to the Caribbean style of Co-Co' observed Steve Priest, who put it down to the fact it was recorded at Island Studios. With more nonsense lyrics about a bloke selling rum cocktails, as with the three previous singles, the band would provide only the vocals, with the usual session crew of Phil Wainman, Pip Williams and John Roberts providing the instrumentation, and Fiachra Trench coming up with the arrangements. Following the relative failure of the previous single, 'Poppa Joe' reached a respectable no. 11 in the UK charts and hit the no. 1 spot in Denmark, Sweden and the Netherlands. However, it no doubt sent a message to Chinn and Chapman that, in the UK at least, the current formula was not going to last forever if they wanted to continue shifting significant quantities of records. Both in the US and the UK, the 'golden age' of bubblegum, if it can be said to have had anything as grand as a golden age, was coming to an end.

The B-side to 'Poppa Joe' was 'Jeanie'. A light acoustic number, more in the vein of 'You're Not Wrong For Loving Me' than many of the band's trademark hard rock B-sides, it had also recently appeared on the debut album.

As well as recording sessions and an ever-expanding round of media appearances, 1972 was also a frenetic year for touring. The Sweet would perform over 120 live gigs during the course of 1972. The band had also sexed up their stage act. The clean-cut image that Connolly had spoken of the previous year had rapidly evolved. The costumes had become wilder, the live act had become raunchier and at a gig in Portsmouth's Mecca Ballroom, in March, the management had taken exception to Connolly's simulated cock-rock playfulness with a microphone and an official marched on stage to stop the show. The incident attracted media attention and The Sweet promptly received a nationwide ban from appearing at any of the Mecca group's venues. The ballroom chain's prudish management, run by Miss World impresario Eric Morley, would inspire the title of a band B-side later in the year.

The notoriety that the band were gaining from their live shows meant things were to take a more dramatic turn when they travelled to Belgium for a gig in Liege in May 1972. Here, they were confronted with a heavy police presence and, immediately following the show, officers made their way backstage and arrested both Connolly and Priest. The former was accused of making obscene gestures with his microphone, while the latter was accused of molesting a female audience member when she came up on stage. The pair spent five days behind bars before appearing in court, where they pleaded not guilty and were subsequently released. Given court proceedings in the Walloon city were obviously conducted in French, what neither the defendants nor anyone connected with the Sweet camp realised was that the pair were only being released on bail and were expected back in court at a later date. In their absence, Connolly and Priest were subsequently handed six-month jail sentences for skipping bail and failing to attend the second hearing. This meant Belgium would be off the band's tour schedule for the foreseeable future. A supportive but not massively significant market for them given Belgium had a population of less than ten million, the band's management were happy to advise them to avoid the country altogether. Chinn: 'It's not Germany. It's not the end of the world if you don't tour Belgium.'

Although it will always be the genre The Sweet will be most strongly associated with, they were neither pioneers of glam rock, in the way that T. Rex or Slade were, nor were they a band whose entire on-stage persona was conceived as a glam rock act from the very start. This was unlike other latecomers to the glam party, such as Gary Glitter and Alvin Stardust, whose identities were developed as glam rock acts from the outset, even though both had had musical careers in previous decades under different names. By mid-1972, The Sweet were an established pop act with four top 40 hits behind them, and neither their bubblegum A-sides nor the band's self-penned hard rock B-sides could reasonably be described in any way as glam rock. One side might sound like The Archies and the other side might sound like Deep Purple, but nowhere did they sound much like the sort of music that Bolan or Bowie or Slade were putting out at the time.

Of course, there are common attributes across both bubblegum and glam. Both emerged as a stark contrast to the countercultural psychedelia of the late 1960s. As culture academic, Philip Auslander (*Performing Glam Rock: Gender and Theatricality in Popular Music,* 2006) argues: 'Whereas psychedelic rock emphasised musical virtuosity and seriousness, glam rock emphasised accessibility and fun.' And what triggered the glam craze in the UK at the start of the 1970s was not a million miles away from what triggered the bubblegum craze in the US at the end of the 1960s. 'When rock went psychedelic and larded down with social statement, up popped bubblegum,' Kim Cooper and David Smay assert in *Bubblegum is the Naked Truth*. Furthermore, as Carl Cafarelli argues in the same volume: 'Glam records were catchy, clunky artificial creations, designed to grab with you with mindless, repetitive and frequently irresistible hooks. It's not a huge jump from Ohio Express to The Sweet, Gary Glitter, Mud, Hello, or even Slade and Suzi Quatro.'

There are also clear differences, though. While bubblegum songs opted for the most simplistic declarations of love, child-like story-telling or fun family games, glam tended to focus far more on those traditional 1950s rock and roll staples: girls, cars, dancing and sex. And while both genres opt for simple melodies and focus on danceability, glam singles were inevitably accompanied by foot-stomping rhythm and loud, raunchy, deafening guitars. Although glam was aimed at singles chart success just as much as bubblegum, it very much saw itself in the rock and roll tradition, not merely as pop music. Moreover, the very theatricality of glam meant there was a focus on the stage personas of glam personalities. This is in marked contrast to the semi-anonymous groups of session men churning out bubblegum.

Single Release
'Little Willy' (Chapman / Chinn) b/w 'Man From Mecca' (Connolly / Priest / Scott / Tucker)

Personnel:
Brian Connolly: lead vocals
Steve Priest: bass guitar, backing vocals
Andy Scott: guitar, backing vocals
Mick Tucker: drums, backing vocals
Additional personnel:
John Roberts: bass
Phil Wainman: drums, percussion
Pip Williams: guitar
Produced at Nova Sound Studios, Island Studios and Central Sound Studios, London, April 1972 by Phil Wainman
UK release date: June 1972
Highest chart places: UK: 4, Germany: 1, US: 3

The Sweet's next single, 'Little Willy' which was released in June 1972, can be seen as something of a glam/bubblegum crossover. Priest: 'Chapman wasn't keen on the tepid buyers' response to 'Poppa Joe'. He decided the next single would be more of a reflection of our B-sides.' Ostensibly about a young man-about-town who likes to stay out late rather than head off home for an early night, the double-entendres in both the lyrics and the title are patently obvious. Scott: 'If the BBC had realised it was that blatant, it would never have got played and would never have been the hit that it was.'

The single had a slightly harder edge, with a prominent guitar line and the faux Latin American rhythms now replaced by a more conventional pop-rock beat. The lyrics, although more risqué, were as inane as ever, however, and once again, it is Wainman's chosen group of session men who got to play on the track, with the four band members only providing vocals. Although the recorded single is somewhat more substantial than previous releases, it is still quite some distance from anything approaching genuine glam rock.

However, it was no long, drawn-out process; The Sweet's metamorphosis from bubblegum act to fully-fledged glam rock stars can be traced back to a single evening: 8 June 1972 – namely their *Top Of The Pops* performance that night. Image-wise it is pretty easy to detect a change in direction, as Scott noted in a later interview (*The Sweet: No Matter What They Say,* Mick Duthie, 2018): 'If it hadn't been for Marc Bolan, I don't think glam would have got off the ground the way it did. He was on *Top Of The Pops* with 'Hot Love' a good six months before we had 'Little Willy', which was our turning point. He had glitter in his hair, on his chest and on his cheeks and makeup that shone. We were stood there in our blue, yellow, red and white outfits looking a bit like the leftovers of a carnival.'

With that in mind, The Sweet are therefore suitably glammed up for their appearance on *Top Of The Pops* performing 'Little Willy', compared to their previous appearance with 'Poppa Joe'. But glam rock is a musical genre first and foremost. If it were just about men in sparkly costumes, then Liberace and every pantomime dame in the land could be categorised as glam rock. So, if we take glam rock to be about sound as well as image, how did The Sweet's metamorphosis come about that night? We have the Musicians' Union to thank for that.

Although guests on the BBC's flagship music show had been miming along to backing tapes since its inception, the broadcaster would insist that, rather than simply mouthing the words to their records, special backing tapes had to be produced for the show. Bands often found ways around this, but when it came to The Sweet's performance of 'Little Willy' the M. U. insisted that the band would not be allowed to mime along to a tape that featured the original single's session players and that if they were appearing on the programme they must record their own backing tape for the show. The M. U.'s ruling had a dramatic impact on what the

Top Of The Pops audience heard that week. Scott's raunchy, fuzzed-up guitar was a seismic improvement on the original and the drumming, which still had little touches of the twee faux-Calypso heard on 'Co-Co' and 'Poppa Joe' here and there, was replaced by Tucker's thudding, glammed-up, echoing beat. In short, in their three-minute slot on the show, the band transformed a fairly lightweight pop song into a genuine, bona fide slice of glam rock. The Sweet's days as a bubblegum band were over. More importantly, the band would play on all of their singles from now on. Their production-cum-management-cum-songwriting team would still remain hugely influential in the day-to-day life of the band, but it would be the authentic sound of The Sweet from now on. Tucker: 'Mike Chapman walked in on us as we were listening to the playback, and his mouth was just hanging open. He heard what we did and he realised we were just as good as the session players, and probably better because we actually cared what the record sounded like and put some of our own personality into it.'

The B-side of 'Little Willy' was 'Man From Mecca', inspired by the band's earlier dealings with the Mecca Leisure Group. With heavy riffing and a glorious Scott solo that could give Led Zeppelin and Deep Purple a run for their money (and which even garnered a glowing review in *Rolling Stone* magazine, no less), the band unleash their fury on what would be their heaviest B-side to date. 'We absolutely had to have a go at the idiot at the last Mecca show,' recalled Priest. 'The song wasn't specifically about him, but the title summed it up and we felt better about the whole incident.'

Single Release
'Wig-Wam Bam' (Chapman / Chinn) b/w **'New York Connection'** (Connolly / Priest / Scott / Tucker)
Personnel:
Brian Connolly: lead vocals
Steve Priest: bass guitar, backing vocals
Andy Scott: guitar, backing vocals
Mick Tucker: drums, backing vocals
Produced at Audio International Studios, London, July 1972 by Phil Wainman
UK release date: September 1972
Highest chart places: UK: 4, Germany: 1, US: Did not chart

The rocked-up, re-tooled version of 'Little Willy' that The Sweet had performed on *Top Of The Pops* now gave Chinn and Chapman a clear template for future releases. The follow-up, 'Wig-Wam Bam', was released on 1 September 1972: 'All handclaps, fat Who-ish chords, compressed drums and stupid words,' as journalist Ken Barnes perfectly describes it. With its pounding tribal drums and raucous fuzzed-up guitar, it became one of the songs that forever helped define the archetypal sound of early 1970s glam rock. Not only was 'Wig-Wam Bam' the first Sweet single from the Chinn and Chapman stable that the band actually played on, finally, it was Chinn and Chapman writing for The Sweet rather than simply writing generic songs that fitted their preconception of what an early 1970s pop band should sound like. 'Wig-Wam Bam' was also notable in being the first single where Priest would deliver his camp semi-spoken-word part, which would go on to become something of a trademark on each of The Sweet's big glam hits. It came about almost by accident. Connolly was struggling with the 'Try a little touch, try a little too much' line and Wainman suggested that Priest have a go instead. 'Mike Chapman was quick to pick up on this and every song after that had a little bit for Steve,' recalled Wainman.

The song returns to the, by now, familiar Chinn-Chapman obsession of native Americans. The lyrics, featuring the likes of Hiawatha, Mini HaHa, Running Bear and Little White Dove, are typical bubblegum fare and no less trite than their predecessors. The raunchy guitar, thunderous rhythm and trademark Sweet vocals, however, instantly make this a glam rock classic, one that can easily sit alongside 'Telegram Sam' and 'Gudbuy T' Jane'. No one listens to glam rock for deep and meaningful lyrics in any case. Reviews were generally positive. *Record Mirror* immediately picked up on the 'heavy basic sound' although *NME* had now decided their love affair with The Sweet had most definitely come to an end. *NME* reviewer, Dennis Holloway, dismissed 'Wig-Wam Bam' in a two-word review as 'unadulterated nonsense'.

'New York Connection' was recorded as the B-side for 'Wig-Wam Bam' and, for once, the crunchy guitar riff which opens the flip-side was not a million miles from that heard on the A-side. For the first time since joining the Chinn-Chapman stable, the single didn't sound like two completely different bands who happened to share the same vocalist. Whereas 'Wig-Wam Bam' was impossibly catchy glam rock with nonsense lyrics, however, 'New York Connection' is a mid-paced hard-rocker with Connolly belting out the vocals in full-on rock-god mode and Scott providing some nice squealing guitar.

As glam's sartorial excesses were becoming ever more pronounced, The Sweet threw themselves in with gusto: 'We've been wearing make-up for ages, which might appear to be conceited,' Connolly explained to *Melody Maker*. 'We're exaggerating it more now with 'Wig-Wam Bam', where the makeup and clothes express the song perfectly. The idea is to put over the camp bit; it's effective and fun to camp it up a bit on stage.' Somewhat paradoxically, however, in that same interview, Connolly also expresses frustration at the band's teenybopper labelling. In an article entitled 'Bitter Sweet' interviewer Mark Plummer wrote: 'It has been suggested to The Sweet that they should play a couple of underground venues where they would be able to reach people outside their usual fan following, but the trouble there — although they would love to play a Roundhouse or Hard-rock gig — is that promoters shy away.' Connolly responded: 'I suppose it's a bit dangerous for promoters to put us on gigs where pop fans are in the minority. We played with Hawkwind at a London college, and one of them came up after our set and was raving about the way we played. We played on their bill, but we went down a bomb.'

Although Belgium was off the tour itinerary, the band's live schedule was taking them further and further afield – including two dates in the Seychelles, where they were booked to perform as part of the week-long Seychelles Festival opened by Princess Margaret, in addition to performances across mainland Europe and the UK.

Album Release
The Sweet's Biggest Hits

Personnel:

Brian Connolly: lead vocals

Steve Priest: bass guitar, backing vocals

Andy Scott: guitars, backing vocals

Mick Tucker: drums, backing vocals

Additional personnel:

John Roberts: bass

Phil Wainman: drums, percussion

Pip Williams: guitar

Fiachra Trench: arrangements

Produced at various London studios, 1970-72 by Phil Wainman

UK release date: December 1972

Highest chart places: UK: Did not chart, Germany: 30, US: Not released

Running time: 36:42
Track listing:
1. Wig-Wam Bam (Chapman / Chinn) 2. Little Willy (Chapman / Chinn) 3. Done Me Wrong Alright (Connolly / Priest / Scott / Tucker) 4. Poppa Joe (Chapman / Chinn) 5. Funny Funny (Chapman / Chinn) 6. Co-Co (Chapman / Chinn) 7. Alexander Graham Bell (Chapman / Chinn) 8. Chop Chop (Chapman / Chinn) 9. You're Not Wrong for Loving Me (Connolly / Priest / Scott / Tucker) 10. Jeanie (Connolly / Priest / Scott / Tucker) 11. Spotlight (Connolly / Priest / Scott / Tucker)

With no new studio album in the offing, RCA brought together The Sweet's six hit singles to date, along with a selection of Connolly-Priest-Scott-Tucker B-sides and Chinn-Chapman's 'Chop Chop' from the *Funny How Sweet…* album and released a compilation aimed at the Christmas market.

The cover carries a large, posed band shot of the four members. Dressed in bright primary colours with not a hint of glitter or silver between them, they look more like children's TV presenters than glam rock stars. The back carries the now-legendary photo of the four dressed in native American costumes, sitting cross-legged on the grass in front of a wig-wam.

The Sweet's Biggest Hits scraped into the top 30 in Germany and reached no. 58 in Australia but failed to chart at all in the UK. In hindsight, it was rather an odd time in the band's career to be issuing a compilation and the resulting album is something of a mixed bag. The Sweet's days of strictly bubblegum hits had come to an end, but the band were only just getting into their stride as a glam rock outfit. Had RCA waited just a few more months and released a hits album in late 1973, as Polydor did with Slade, for example, it would have been a much more impressive and substantial affair. Indeed, Polydor's own *Sladest* compilation, which brought together Slade's glam hits along with some pre-fame earlier material, rocketed to no. 1 in September 1973.

1972 was still quite a year, though. The Sweet had started the year off singing along to bubblegum backing tracks made by session men and ended it as true glam rock icons.

Chapter Five: 1973 – Blockbuster, Hellraiser and Blitz

If the 1970s were glam's decade, then 1973 was certainly glam's year. Not only did The Sweet have hits with 'Blockbuster!', 'Hell Raiser' and 'Ballroom Blitz', they were joined by Slade ('Cum On Feel The Noize', 'Skweeze Me Pleeze Me', 'My Friend Stan', 'Merry Xmas Everybody'); Gary Glitter ('Do You Wanna Touch Me', 'Hello Hello I'm Back Again', 'I'm The Leader of The Gang (I Am)', 'I Love You Love Me Love'); T. Rex ('20th Century Boy, 'The Groover'); Suzi Quatro ('Can The Can', '48 Crash') and Mud ('Dynamite') all of which made the UK top five at various point in the year. The Sweet had successfully made the transition from bubblegum pop to glam rock. 'In the early days, we even used to be put in the same bag as Middle Of The Road,' Scott told *NME* that year. 'We were a bunch of wankers who didn't play on their backing tracks. I think we've lived that one down now.'

Of course, there was nothing at all unusual in those who would end up as glam rockers making various attempts to enjoy a breakthrough in other musical genres long before glam came along. Indeed, this was the pattern with virtually everyone involved in the first couple of waves of glam rock acts. Marc Bolan and David Bowie had each started out as part of the London mod scene, both releasing debut singles in the mid-1960s R&B boom and then being part of the countercultural hippy acoustic scene prior to becoming glam pioneers. Slade's pre-glam recording debut also came in the 1960s with a soulful cover of the Young Rascals' 'You Better Run' in 1966 while Gary Glitter's first single, a crooning ballad titled 'Alone In The Night' under the stage-name of Paul Raven, had been released as far back as 1960. His backing band, The Glitter Band, meanwhile had begun life in 1966 as The Boston Show Band.

Neither was there any shortage of musicians who had been involved in the bubblegum craze but had subsequently moved on to pastures new. In the US, prime bubblegum outfit the 1910 Fruitgum Company (who had a worldwide smash in 1968 with 'Simon Says' followed by a string of bubblegum hits) attempted a change in direction worthy of Spinal Tap when they donned biker leathers, cranked up the guitars and delivered an album of experimental hard rock. In the UK, meanwhile, all four members of the original line-up of 10cc hooked up with US-based bubblegum writers and producers Jerry Kasenetz and Jeffry Katz to record a string of formulaic bubblegum singles that were released under a variety of names.

However, The Sweet were pretty unique in making the transition from successful bubblegum act to successful glam rock act – and that is before we even contemplate their later career.

Nevertheless, 1973 started off as something of a PR disaster for The Sweet. To launch their latest single, the band were booked into the legendary Ronnie Scott's jazz venue in London's Soho to perform in front of the assembled music press. Sound and equipment problems conspired to mar the band's performance. The *NME's* Nick Kent, never needing much of an excuse to run down The Sweet, was later to describe it as 'the worst group performance to be allowed on stage since the discovery of electricity'. An extraordinary and quite weird coincidence would also lead to further sneering in the music press. In January 1973, two singles released by RCA with instantly memorable but remarkably similar riffs were both enjoying chart success: The Sweet's 'Blockbuster!' and David Bowie's 'The Jean Genie'.

Single Release
'Blockbuster!' (Chapman / Chinn) b/w **'Need A Lot Of Lovin''** (Connolly / Priest / Scott / Tucker)
Personnel:
Brian Connolly: lead vocals
Steve Priest: bass guitar, backing vocals
Andy Scott: guitar, backing vocals
Mick Tucker: drums, backing vocals
Produced at Audio International Studios, London. November 1972 by Phil Wainman
UK release date: January 1973
Highest chart places: UK: 1, Germany: 1, US: 73

'Blockbuster!' began life while 'Wig-Wam Bam' was still climbing the charts. Chapman presented it to The Sweet as his idea for the next single while they were backstage at the BBC waiting to enter the *Top Of The Pops* studio to perform 'Wig-Wam Bam'. This is most likely to be the band's first of three appearances promoting 'Wig-Wam Bam' on the show, broadcast on 14 September 1972. Priest: 'While we were sitting in the TV studio's dressing room waiting for our call, Mike pulled out his acoustic and played us a riff. It sounded a bit like 'I'm A Man' by Bo Diddley. Sounding much different from anything else he had ever played us. It caught our attention.'

Recorded on 1 November 1972 at London's Audio International Studios, The Sweet's 'Blockbuster!' was released the following January. The distinctive siren intro was Wainman's inspired idea. In interviews at the time, band members were all enthusiastic about this latest single. Scott discussed in *Disc* magazine in 1972: 'We're getting more adventurous with our singles. Our next one, 'Blockbuster', is a rock song, nobody could call it bubblegum.' Connolly said in *Creem* magazine in 1973): 'Chapman and Chinn wanted a single that was more representative of the Sweet as we perform. They follow us; they don't guide us.' Tucker said in the same piece: 'We can't write 'Blockbuster'. We've tried. We've written the B-sides of our records, but we can't write hits, at least not right now.'

The riff was remarkably similar to David Bowie's 'The Jean Genie', however, recorded on 6 October 1972 and released in November 1972. At the end of September 1972, Bowie and The Spiders had played three dates in the US: Cleveland on 22nd, Memphis on 24th and New York on 28th. In Paul Trynka's Bowie biography *Starman,* he recounts how, fired up by the legacy of Elvis Presley and Muddy Waters on reaching Memphis, the riff of Waters' 'I'm A Man' emerged during an impromptu tour bus jam. Bowie started strumming along, recounted bass player Trevor Bolder, 'and then he wrote the song'. Certainly, by the time he reached New York, Bowie had developed a complete set of lyrics. By 6 October, Bowie had told his bandmates that the song would be the next single and they went into RCA's New York Studios that very day to lay it down in a couple of takes. Bowie's 'Jean Genie' was released on 25 November.

Although it seems an incredible coincidence that two different artists both contracted to the same record label would each record and release singles with virtually identical riffs at around the same time completely independently of one another in two different continents, that is exactly what happened. While Bowie was the first to get his song recorded and released, Chapman was presenting his new composition to The Sweet in the UK a good few days before the tour bus jam in the US that inspired Bowie to start writing 'The Jean Genie'. Chapman told *NME* later that year: 'We wrote the song in September. When I was thinking of the basic theme, I was going da-da-da-dumm-dumm, thinking: Oh yeah, the Nashville Teens' 'Tobacco Road'.' Chinn: 'The ridiculous thing was, of course, they were both on the same record label. But I know we never heard Bowie's 'Jean Genie' and to the best of my knowledge he hadn't heard 'Blockbuster!''

The coincidence was not lost on Scott either: 'And then, you wouldn't believe this, before our release we were in the office of the guy who was our contact at RCA and he played us the new David Bowie record, he played us 'Jean Genie'. And I went, 'That's the same guitar riff,' and he went, 'Is it?' This is a record company guy and I'm saying, 'Haven't you noticed?' And he went, 'No.' I was horrified, I was thinking: that's coming out first, and we're coming out a week behind it, on the same label, it's got the same guitar riff. I said: well, we don't stand a chance of being #1. That was my thought. And within three weeks, we were #1 and he was #2.'

In what is thought to be Connolly's last interview before he died, the singer relayed his own 'Blockbuster!' recollections to journalist Jasper Rees: '...when we took the acetate into the promotion department at RCA for the first time to let them hear what their next single was going to be, Bowie was in that promotion department. I remember him saying, 'That's a great song, that's definitely a winner.''

This is clearly implausible, however. Bowie was touring the States throughout the Autumn of 1972 and did not return to the UK until December, long after 'Jean Genie' had been written, recorded and released and several weeks after 'Blockbuster!' had been recorded. There was simply no way that Bowie was popping into RCA's London offices during this time to listen to 'Blockbuster!' or anything else for that matter.

Regardless of the origins of the riff, however, it remains one hell of a record, one of the most memorable and definitive songs of the entire glam era and, indeed, one of the greatest singles of all time. From the sirens to the riff to Priest's outrageously camp spluttering interjections, everything about the recording is perfection. The public agreed. 'Blockbuster!' climbed to no. 1 in the UK charts where it would spend some five weeks, the band's only chart-topper on home territory. Bowie's 'Jean Genie' meanwhile nestled at no. 2. Those glam rock adaptations of that old blues riff were certainly proving popular. Internationally, 'Blockbuster!' was a top-five hit across much of Europe as well as New Zealand. It failed to make much of an impact in the United States, however, reaching just a lowly no. 73 in the Billboard charts when it was released by Bell. It would take a new record company for the band to really start having an impact in the US.

While 'Blockbuster!' was one of the very pinnacles for early 1970s glam rock, 'Need A Lot Of Lovin'', meanwhile, followed the template the band had established for their self-composed B-sides: loud, mean, uncompromising hard rock. Described as 'out-purpling Deep Purple' by Ken Barnes of *Phonograph* magazine, the song starts out with a riff that is reminiscent of a heavy metal version of 'Wig-Wam Bam' and then becomes a showcase for a demonic bass-line from Priest, some powerhouse drumming from Tucker, some furiously-debauched lyrics from Connolly, and a magnificent guitar solo from Scott. It can easily stand up against tracks from any number of classic albums from leading hard rock acts of the day.

Ahead of the release of their next single, 'Hell Raiser', the band embarked on a UK tour in late March 1973 and, just as with the press launch for 'Blockbuster!' a couple of months earlier, the band had another PR disaster to contend with. A gig was scheduled at the prestigious London rock venue, The Rainbow, the setting for many iconic live albums of the period. Key figures from the music press were invited, once again, and it would be a chance to showcase the band's credentials as an energetic and talented live rock outfit, rather than as mere purveyors of glam and bubblegum hits. Unfortunately, disaster was to strike once more. There were sound problems right from the start and then just a few songs into the show, the PA system blew altogether. Desperately scrabbling around to save the night, Connolly eventually managed to find a microphone that worked and the band ploughed on with an acoustic run-through of their main hits. Credible rock showcase this was not. The reviews were predictably scathing. James Johnson of the *NME*, obviously on the lookout for a colourful put-down to rival Nick Kent's at the start of the year, was later to write that the band, 'managed to bomb out on a scale almost unparalleled since the Titanic's maiden voyage.'

It was Charles Shaar Murray, however, who was to review the gig for the *NME* that night, writing: 'The Sweet are an exceptionally unexceptional band who've been lucky enough to get a solid string of instant hit songs of such banal simplicity that they've become hits. They play to an audience of rather unimaginative eight-to-sixteen-year-olds, and what they play is a clumsy parody of what rock music is really about.'

Ray Fox Cumming of *Disc* magazine was no more favourable: 'The quality of the sound, Wainman or no Wainman, was definitely not too hot, something approximately like an 8,000-watt Woolworths transistor radio, at such a volume level that individual sounds are hardly discernible. Behind it all is the kind of cheesy noise produced by any very average heavy band in a bad mood.'

Single Release
'Hell Raiser' (Chapman / Chinn) b/w 'Burning' (Connolly / Priest / Scott / Tucker)

Personnel:

Brian Connolly: lead vocals

Steve Priest: bass guitar, backing vocals

Andy Scott: guitar, backing vocals

Mick Tucker: drums, backing vocals

Produced at Audio International Studios, London, March 1973 by Phil Wainman

UK release date: April 1973

Highest chart places: UK: 2, Germany: 1, US: Not released

Despite the Rainbow fiasco, the band bounced back with the release of 'Hell Raiser'. Beginning with an almighty yell (a cameo appearance from Chapman) followed by the sound of a huge explosion, 'Hell Raiser' is certainly the most aggressive sounding of the three Sweet singles that were released during the course of 1973. With a choppy, heavy metal-style riff and some exhilaratingly wild vocals from Connolly, along with monster sounding drums from Tucker, it is a single that more closely matches the type of hard rock material the band were putting out on the B-sides. Chinn said in a *Glitz, Blitz & Hitz,* interview in 2003: ''Hell Raiser' didn't get written by accident. Hellraisers is exactly what Sweet were.' Wainman later contended that it was more heavy rock than glam rock and that the band 'really wanted to be Deep Purple relived.'

It was no surprise that the song was later covered by heavy metal bands like Raven when the New Wave Of British Heavy Metal (NWOBHM) scene started up a few years later. However, when the band first heard an acoustic demo of the song (sent over by Chapman while they were on tour in Hong Kong) they did not quite know what to make of it and apparently 'fell on the floor laughing' when the tape was first played. It was only when they got back to London and began rehearsing the song prior to visiting Audio International Studios to make the recording that the song, as we know it, really began to take shape. Priest: 'Luckily, when we got together with Mike, he explained his whole idea of the song to us and it all came together.'

The B-side was another group composition: 'Burning'. The idea for the song originated while the band were in rehearsals on their recent tour. Beginning with Scott unleashing some frenetic soloing on his guitar and followed through with a powerful chugging riff and those trademark harmonised vocals, all the key ingredients for yet another impressive Sweet

B-side appear to be falling into place. Coming up with actual lyrics for this new song, however, would prove to be a little more problematic and the source of some tensions within the band. Connolly had been afforded the responsibility of writing some. What emerged, though, was deemed to be a little on the thin side to fill out a full song and producer, Wainman, padded out the gaps with sound effects. These took the form of the (then) instantly recognisable telephone speaking clock, familiar to anyone in the UK at the time who dialled up, along with some wickedly manic laughter. Although such audio gimmicks make for a memorable track, the band subsequently felt they could do far more with the riff, and it would evolve into a different song entirely: 'Someone Else Will'. In the band's live sets, 'Burning' and 'Someone Else Will' would end up being played as a medley. 'Someone Else Will' on its own would eventually turn up as the B-side to the ill-fated 'Turn It Down' single a year later.

'Hell Raiser' was another no. 2 hit for The Sweet in the UK, a no. 1 in both Denmark and Germany and top five in several other countries. The reviews, however, were the usual mixed bag. *Record Mirror* correctly predicted it would be another chart giant and commended its commanding tempo and catchy chorus hook. Charles Shaar Murray in the *NME*, once again, was characteristically dismissive: 'Phase Two in The Sweet's campaign to be recognised and respected by the Heavy Metal Mob. It starts out with a scream and an atomic explosion and degenerates from there. The back-up is tight but unadventurous, and Connolly's ham-fisted version of Bowie's vocal mannerisms successfully precludes any chance of appreciative listening.'

Although there would be no UK album from The Sweet in 1973, the band's initial US label Bell issued a compilation album in the summer simply entitled *The Sweet*. This drew together the last four UK singles ('Little Willy', 'Wig-Wam Bam', 'Blockbuster!' and 'Hell Raiser') along with a selection of B-sides. Reviewer Jon Tiven, writing for *Zoo World*, rightly concluded that this compilation was a much superior effort to the UK's own *The Sweet's Biggest Hits*, arguing: 'The Sweet are masters of the 3:25 minute song, never overextending themselves into concept albums or anything that would deter them from their proper course. Right on, boys!'

Single Release
'The Ballroom Blitz' (Chapman / Chinn) b/w 'Rock & Roll Disgrace' (Connolly / Priest / Scott / Tucker)

Personnel:
Brian Connolly: lead vocals

Steve Priest: bass guitar, backing vocals
Andy Scott: guitar, backing vocals
Mick Tucker: drums, backing vocals
Produced at Audio International Studios, London, June 1973 by Phil Wainman
UK release date: September 1973
Highest chart places: UK: 2, Germany: 1, US: 5

With its unmistakeable signature beat, ludicrously camp spoken intro
and manically delivered chorus, 'The Ballroom Blitz' is one of the most
memorable Sweet songs of all time. Recorded in June 1973 at Audio
International Studios, it was released in September as the third in the
triumvirate of era-defining singles by the band over the course of 1973.
Chapman: 'We were trying to write songs that had no meaning, and
'Ballroom Blitz' was one of them. I suggested the title, and we sat down
and wrote a song about a guy having a horrifyingly bad dream that his
latest record hadn't made it – he was in this ballroom, in a discotheque,
and maybe he was on drugs because he started hallucinating.' Scott, in an
interview on thesweet.com in 2010: 'Mike Chapman came up to see us
in Glasgow… and what he saw at this ballroom was mayhem. Brian and
I both ended up in the audience. Girls with scissors trying to cut your
hair and all this kind of stuff going on. And he just said it was blitz. It was
blitzkrieg. And he wrote 'The Ballroom Blitz' the next day.'

For the song's iconic drumbeat, Priest credits Wainman in coming up
with that and recalled that the band sat around in rehearsals trying to
think of something that would make Chinn and Chapman's rough outline
for the song come alive. Wainman eventually got out a pair of drumsticks
and started tapping out the rhythm to 'Let There Be Drums', a song by
legendary drummer Sandy Neilson. The Sweet immediately had their
special ingredient. Priest: 'Without Phil, 'Ballroom Blitz' would have
sounded like a weak Marc Bolan reject.' In their drummer, of course, The
Sweet also had their own special secret weapon to bring that rhythm to
life. Scott: 'I am still yet to hear another drummer play that intro like Mick
played it.'

The B-side was another band composition, 'Rock & Roll Disgrace',
which had been written a few weeks prior to recording. Another Zeppelin-
esque slice of infectious heavy rock with raw riffs, tongue-in-cheek lyrics,
campy interjections and classic Sweet harmonies, it was another worthy
flip-side that showcased the band's hard rock credentials.

The 'Ballroom Blitz' single sold spectacularly well but was kept off the top slot in the UK by the surprise orchestral novelty hit 'Eye Level' by the Simon Park Orchestra, theme to the popular TV crime series *Van der Valk*. Nevertheless, it was a top five hit internationally, including a no. 1 in Australia, Canada, Denmark, Germany and New Zealand. Crucially, while it would not be a hit there for another two years, it would also reach no. 5 in the US Billboard charts, a significant commercial breakthrough for the band at a time when little had been heard of them since the days of 'Little Willy'. In later years, the song was covered by UK punk outfit The Damned in 1979 (with Motörhead's Lemmy guesting on bass), Swiss heavy metal band Krokus (who named their 1984 album *The Blitz* in homage to the Sweet classic) and US actress/singer Tia Carrere (who performed the song for the soundtrack of the 1992 film *Wayne's World)*.

While The Sweet had chalked up three spectacular glam singles during the course of 1973, there was still no sign of a new album since the release of the decidedly patchy *Funny How Sweet Co-Co Can Be* back in 1971. Earlier in the year, Scott had enthused about a new album in the making when interviewed by *Disc* magazine, telling Ray Fox-Cumming in February 1973:

> It's already about half-written. The four of us, Brian, Steve, Mick and myself, are working with Nicky and Mike to compose the songs. It's going to be a concept album relating to Rock-n-Roll over a 20-year period, with the songs possibly joined together with monologue – we're not sure about that yet. Each of the songs will relate to a two-year period – although we won't date them, in case we might be a bit out! We're not aiming for authenticity of sound. It will be the Sweet sound, but we hope that people will be reminded of something from the era we're relating to just by the flavour of the song.

By September, however, Tucker was telling James Johnson of the *NME* that the concept had been abandoned: 'We were going to make our next album a sort of 'History of Rock', but a couple of other people beat us to it so the idea's been shelved. Rigor Mortis have done it now, and Bowie has, so we thought if we went ahead the headlines would read 'Sweet rip off everybody'. Now the album is just going to be our own songs.'

Just one track from the abandoned *History of Rock* project would see the light of day. This was a cover of 'Peppermint Twist' that was originally a US Billboard No. 1 hit for Joey Dee & The Starlighters back in 1961. It would be released as a track on the *Sweet Fanny Adams* album the following year, but, for now, Sweet fans would have to wait. Given that any number of their contemporaries had several albums behind them at this stage, questions were starting to be asked in the music press about when a Sweet album might materialise, particularly given it was frequently noted that the band did not write their own singles. In an article entitled 'Can You Take The Sweet Seriously?' an uncredited writer in *Beat Instrumental* opined: 'You may think I'm being very unfair – but you must admit that having had nine hit singles in Britain, all penned by Chinn and Chapman and blatantly designed for the singles charts, it is very hard to take Sweet seriously, as far as albums go.'

However, the writer did go on to acknowledge the strength of the band's self-written B-sides and, with a considerable degree of accuracy, suggested these may provide an indication as to what a future Sweet album may sound like:

> Don't think that this album is going to be Sweet's first attempt at songwriting. If you flip over any of the nine hit singles that they've released, you'll see that Sweet have already been busying themselves writing the B-sides. And if you listen to those B-sides, you'll notice that Sweet, as songwriters, have totally different ideas from Chinn and Chapman as far as their music goes. Listening to those B-sides will probably give you some idea of what to expect on their forthcoming album.

Although not quite as frantic as the previous year, The Sweet would still play almost 100 live gigs during the course of 1973, including frequent trips to the continent as well as a tour that took in New Zealand, Australia and Hong Kong, on top of several tours of the UK. After experiencing what *Beat Instrumental* described as being 'left on stage looking like a primary school band at an end-of-term dance', The Sweet tempted fate once more and returned to London's Rainbow on 21 December to perform their final gig of the year, a rescheduled date following the earlier fiasco. Finally, this one was to proceed without mishap. Indeed, audio and film footage of the gig was captured for posterity.

Filmed excerpts from the concert would appear on a BBC documentary early the following year, while some of the soundtrack would materialise as one half of the two-disc *Strung Up* album released in 1975. However, the gremlins that bedevilled the previous Rainbow gig did not disappear entirely. Although the concert itself proceeded without a hitch, there were technical flaws in the sound recording which resulted in parts of

Tucker's drums not being properly recorded. Tucker laid down some additional overdubs and, initially, just seven tracks from the concert were made publicly available when *Strung Up* released. However, a recording of the full concert was subsequently released on CD in 1999. Even though only the mono versions of the original tapes could be located and even though the film footage (apart from those few excerpts used by the BBC) has never been found, the live album of The Rainbow gig nevertheless provides an excellent record of a Sweet gig around that time.

Opening with a tape of 'The Stripper' played over the PA, the band's traditional walk-on theme, the four launch into an incendiary rendition of 'Hell Raiser'. The other key glam-era, post-bubblegum hit singles get an airing, along with a preview of the band's next single, 'Teenage Rampage' which would be released in early 1974. A good proportion of the set-list, however, is given over to the self-penned hard rock B-sides, including the 'Burning / Someone Else Will' medley that was now an essential component of the band's live act. In addition, there is an epic thirteen-minute-long rendition of Elmer Bernstein's 'The Man With The Golden Arm' where, after another taped intro, the band launch into their own heavy metal interpretation before Tucker lets rip with a mammoth drum solo. The live recording also includes a thrillingly vibrant rock'n'roll medley, pulling in the likes of 'Keep A Knockin', 'Lucille' and 'Great Balls Of Fire'. This is only marred by some rather unfortunate alternative lyrics for an otherwise exhilarating version of 'Reelin' And Rockin', which, sadly, cross the line from cocky, rock'n'roll debauchery into outright violent misogyny. A parent would not have had to have been in league with Mary Whitehouse to have had some concerns about their young teenybopper offspring hearing lyrics such as these. Indeed, one of the reviews at the time characterised the evening as 'slick but sleazy'.

That aside, it is interesting nonetheless how much more delightfully raucous and fizzing with energy the band's 1950s rock'n'roll renditions have become by this stage, when compared to the more restrained offerings on the Swedish radio broadcast two years earlier. Scott was later to describe the December Rainbow gig as one of the best the band ever played. The live recording is certainly a powerful record of a band at its peak.

The Sweet rounded off 1973 with a memorable appearance on the Christmas Day *Top Of The Pops*. Broadcast on 25 December and recorded several days earlier, it is the one where Priest made his infamous appearance as a camp, dragged-up Nazi stormtrooper, replete with

Swastika armband. It is unimaginable that any rock band would attempt
to go on mainstream national television in such a get-up these days
but flirting with Nazi imagery was actually quite common in the 1970s,
including in the punk era a few years later. In hindsight, with both the
glam and punk contexts (and with Basil Fawlty in *Fawlty Towers* for that
matter!), it can be seen as far more about mocking the older war-time
generation and stuffy establishment attitudes rather than about trivialising
the atrocities of the Nazi era. It is not something any self-respecting
band would want to repeat nowadays, but at the time, it was a suitably
outrageous, fun and irreverent end to the year.

1973 would be glam rock's absolute zenith – and The Sweet's for that
matter: three of the most memorable singles the band would ever record,
their first and only UK number one and, while the costumes were getting
sillier, the singles were becoming a more authentic representation of what
the band were really about, the sound was getting rockier and record
sales were soaring. The Sweet were still to release an album that in any
way represented the band's sound – but 1974 was just around the corner.

Chapter Six: 1974 – Two Classic Albums

If The Sweet were to transcend characterisation as a singles act and secure recognition as artists who could also produce great rock albums, it certainly took a long time for that evidence to materialise. By early 1974, T. Rex had released their fifth album (their ninth if you include the Tyrannosaurus Rex ones), Slade were also onto their fifth, whereas a genuinely album-orientated act like Deep Purple were now on their tenth. All The Sweet had managed to get into the twelve-inch racks at this point were the very patchy *Funny How Sweet...* and a couple of hastily thrown together compilations. Over the course of the year, however, the band would rectify this by releasing not one but two classic albums. Many fans would maintain that the two albums in question remain the two strongest of the band's career. First, however, there would be another glam rock single, another no.2 chart placing and a very unfortunate injury for Brian Connolly.

Single Release
'Teenage Rampage' (Chapman / Chinn) b/w 'Own Up, Take A Look At Yourself' (Connolly / Priest / Scott / Tucker)

Personnel:

Brian Connolly: lead vocals

Steve Priest: bass guitar, backing vocals

Andy Scott: guitar, backing vocals

Mick Tucker: drums, backing vocals

Produced at Audio International Studios, London, November 1973 by Phil Wainman

UK release date: January 1974

Highest chart places: UK: 2, Germany: 1, US: Did not chart

The Sweet's first single of the year, released in January 1974, was the Chinn-Chapman penned 'Teenage Rampage'. This followed a gap of several months since the last of their great triumvirate of 1973 singles: 'Blockbuster!', 'Hell Raiser' and 'Ballroom Blitz'. In actual fact, another song, 'Dynamite', was mooted as the follow-up to 'Ballroom Blitz' but passed over and then recorded but not released by up-coming glam band Hello. It was finally released by Mud, who sent it to a very respectable no. 4 in the UK charts. A glam gothic horror-themed ditty 'Moonlight In Baskerville' was then offered to The Sweet, but that, too, was eventually rejected. Chapman then turned up with 'Teenage Rampage'. The latter was certainly more anthemic than either 'Dynamite' or 'Moonlight in Baskerville' (for which a Mike Chapman unreleased demo recording can be found on YouTube).

'Teenage Rampage' was one of a several singles that celebrated the power of the teenager around that time, including T. Rex's 'Teenage Dream' and Alice Cooper's 'Teenage Lament 74'. With its Nuremberg-style chanting and screaming dubbed intro, it was certainly memorable and outrageously over the top but perhaps lacks the class of its three glam predecessors. As with Slade's 'Skweeze Me Pleeze Me', which reached no. 1 a few months earlier (but was never quite in the same class as their previous hits like 'Cum On Feel The Noize), perhaps it was a sign that things were getting just a little *too* bombastic, even for glam. Scott: 'We felt it was a slightly backwards step after 'Ballroom Blitz'.'

The mood of rebellion enshrined in 'Teenage Rampage' clearly found a captive audience, though. Following industrial action by mineworkers in late 1973, the UK government had introduced a three-day working week in January 1974 to preserve coal stocks. There were frequent power cuts and TV stations closed down early to encourage everyone to save fuel and have an early night. Even though *NME* slammed the single as 'a horrible record' and condemned its 'phoney music and phoney politics', the fans thought differently. 'I think 'Teenage Rampage' by the Sweet is great,' Linda Perkins (17) of Cardiff told the same paper in February 1974. 'Not only because I love Sweet but because it speaks of a revolution of the teenage set over the older generation.' TV clean-up campaigner, Mary Whitehouse, did not see things in the same way at all. In a hilarious exchange of letters between Whitehouse and the BBC's Head of Radio that eventually saw publication in 2012, Whitehouse had demanded that the broadcaster ban 'Teenage Rampage' from the airwaves, arguing:

> I am writing with regard to a 'pop' record currently being played on radio, namely, 'TEENAGE RAMPAGE' sung by SWEET. The words include the following: 'All over the land the kids are out to get the upper hand, They're out on the streets, to turn on the heat, And soon they'll be completely in command…'. Yesterday I rang your duty officer about the matter and asked that it should be brought to your attention immediately. I hope you will agree that the playing of such a record is wholly inadvisable in present circumstances and look forward to hearing that you have seen fit to ban any further transmission of this record.

Right: The Sweet's debut single 'Slow Motion' released in 1968. (*Michael Mandt*)

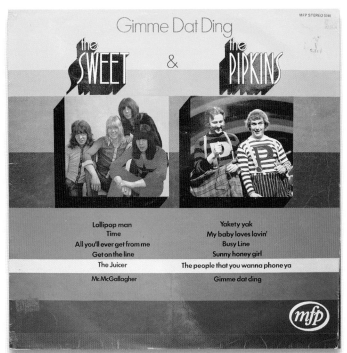

Left: *Gimme Dat Ding*. Before their debut album was out, their old record company rush-released a tacky compilation. (*Universal*)

Left: A curious mixture of bubblegum, cabaret and hard rock – *Funny How Sweet Co-Co Can Be*, 1971. (*Sony*)

Right: Looking more like children's TV presenters than glam rock stars – *The Sweet's Biggest Hits*, 1972. (*Sony*)

Right: *Sweet Fanny Adams,* 1974. Scott: 'Full of energy, humour and social statement of the era'. (*Sony*)

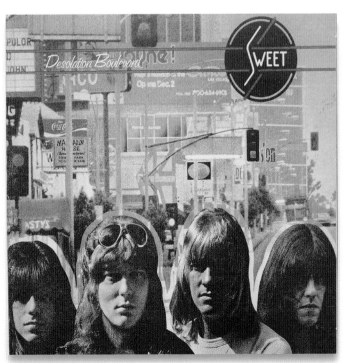

Left: *Desolation Boulevard,* 1974. If you only own one Sweet album, this is the 'must-have'. (*Sony*)

Above: 'We want to prove to people that we're versatile and not a bubblegum group'. A publicity photo from 1971.

Below: Andy Scott on *Top of the Pops* in 1975.

Right: The teen pin-up years. Brian Connolly on the cover of *Tina* magazine, November 1973. (*Michael Mandt*)

Left: Steve Priest also gets the teen pin-up treatment in *Music Star* magazine. (*Michael Mandt*)

RECORD, FUNNY - FUNNY NOW AT
30 IN THE CHARTS, AND GOING UP FAST.

APPEARING

ON WEDNESDAY MARCH 17

MEMBERS 75p.   GUESTS 100p

PRESENTED BY GERRY EDWIN ENTERTAINMENTS.

TEL N/A 3363

FREE! Transport from Northallerton – 8p.m. – 8-30p.m. & 9p.m.
outside Uptons.

Left: The band's live schedule ramped up considerably after Scott joined them. A March 1971 concert flyer. (*Michael Mandt*)

Above: 'We've been wearing make-up for ages'. A 1972 tour souvenir. (*Michael Mandt*)

DOME - BRIGHTON

Thursday, November 29
at 8 pm

PETER ROBINSON and JOHN LEIGH present
IN CONCERT

THE SWEET

and SUN CHARIOT

Tickets: £1.40, £1.25 and £1.10 from Dome box office, New Road, Brighton. Tel. 682127

An Amicus presentation

Left: Tour publicity for a Brighton Dome gig on 29 November 1973. (*Michael Mandt*)

Above: 'An album far, far better than I, for one, would have ever believed them capable.' *Disc* magazine, talking about *Sweet Fanny Adams* in 1974. (*Michael Mandt*)

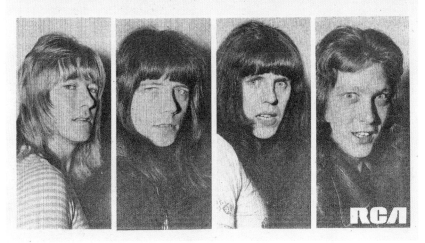

Above: A proud record company congratulate The Sweet. An RCA press advert. (*Michael Mandt*)

Left: *Strung Up* in 1975. Joe Petagno's gatefold cover demonstrates that Sweet were nobody's puppets. (*Sony*)

Right: 'Queen are a bunch of Winkers!' the graffiti-strewn cover for *Give Us A Wink* in 1976. (*Sony*)

Right: You can almost sense the cocaine oozing from its tracks. *Off the Record* in 1977. (*Sony*)

Above: The inner gatefold cover art for the beautifully packaged *Off The Record* album. (*Sony*)

BLOCKBUSTER / HELL RAISER
BALLROOM BLITZ / LOST ANGELS
TEENAGE RAMPAGE / SIX TEENS
TURN IT DOWN / ACTION
FOX ON THE RUN / FEVER OF LOVE
LIES IN YOUR EYES

Left: RCA's parting shot prior to a switch of record labels. *The Golden Greats* hits compilation from 1977. (*Sony*)

Right: Quite unlike any Sweet album that had gone before it – *Level Headed* from 1978. (*Universal*)

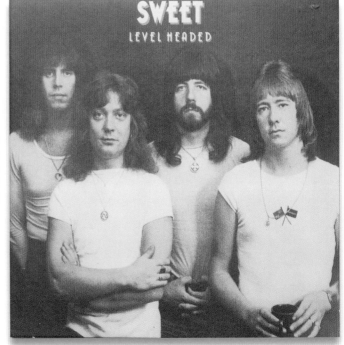

Right: The first album without Brian Connolly – *Cut Above the Rest* from 1979. (*Universal*)

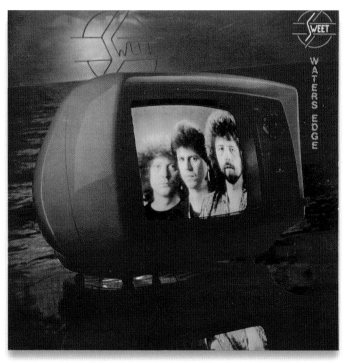

Left: One cannot help feeling that things have started to come full circle. *Water's Edge* in 1980. (*Universal*)

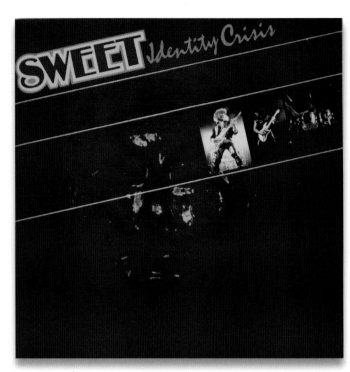

Left: Scott: 'We're gonna forget the corn and blatant commerciality and get something a bit rawer'. *Identity Crisis*, 1982. (*Universal*)

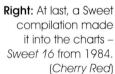

Right: At last, a Sweet compilation made it into the charts – *Sweet 16* from 1984. (*Cherry Red*)

Right: The December 1973 Rainbow gig – 'one of the best the band ever played'. (*Sony*)

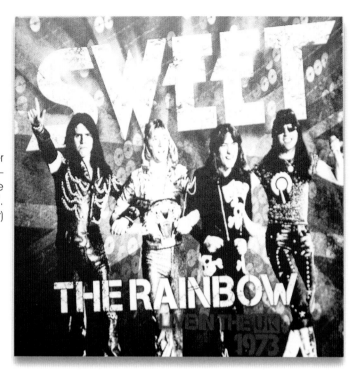

Left: Frequent visitors to the BBC's Maida Vale studios at the start of the 1970s, *The Sweet at the Beeb* in 2017. (*Sony*)

BYE BYE BRIAN!

Connolly leaves Sweet

BRIAN CONNOLLY has left Sweet after long discussions about their musical direction.

He has been trying different experiments with the band who have been together for ten years, but their ideas have not been compatible.

And the move has been made harder because of the success of their last album, 'Level Headed'.

But now Connolly will go into the studio to start work on his own solo album, tentatively titled 'A Cut Above The Rest'.

His manager, David Walker said: "Brian was a teenybop idol. But as you grow up you change your attitudes and you want to do something different."

The rest of the band will also go into the studios to work on their own album.

Sweet loses Connolly

SWEET KEYBOARDS player Brian Connolly is leaving the band after almost ten years, in order to concentrate on a solo recording career. However, manager David Walker, head of Handle Artists, emphasised that Connolly's departure did not signal the end of Sweet as either a touring or recording outfit.

Walker told *Music Week*: "Quite simply, Brian Connolly feels that his future lies in a different direction to that of the remaining Sweet members, Mick Tucker, Steve Priest and Andy Scott. I know that he hasn't been all that happy since Sweet changed their musical image from teenybop to more heavy rock, because he sees himself more as a country rock performer."

> **Edited by CHRIS WHITE**

Connolly was one of the founder members of Sweet back in 1968 — the group had a string of teenybop hits originating from Nicky Chinn and Mike Chapman and total world record sales to date are more than 35 million units. Two years ago the band signed with Polydor and had a worldwide hit with Love Is Like Oxygen.

A new Sweet single, Call Me, the first since Connolly left the group, is released later this month followed by an album, A Cut Above The Rest, in March. Meanwhile Connolly — who will continue to be managed by Walker — will be going into the studios shortly, to record a solo single.

"It is more than possible that the other members of Sweet will have some involvement with his recordings and we are hoping that Pip Williams will also be able to do some production work with him," said Walker.

Walker also admitted: "It is true that Sweet will lose a very visual frontman, and perhaps a certain identity, but I think that they will also gain something else in the process — it will allow their personalities to come to the fore. Similarly the situation will also allow Brian to develop as an artist."

Three-piece Sweet!

CONNOLLY OPTS OUT

THE SWEET are down to a three-piece unit following the departure, after ten years, of singer Brian Connolly who's decided to pursue a solo career. The remaining three members — Andy Scott (guitar), Steve Priest (bass) and Mick Tucker (drums) — are not going to replace him, and will in future share vocal honours.

This new trio format can be heard initially on a new single titled 'Call Me', for Polydor release on March 2. And this will be followed in April by an album called 'A Cut Above The Rest'. They have no immediate plans for live dates, but a spokesman said they will probably do a few selected gigs at the time of the LP's release.

The Sweet enjoyed enormous success in the first half of the '70s, notably in the singles charts with a string of ten successive hits, including a No. 1 with 'Blockbuster'. They've tended to fade out of the picture more recently, though this could partially be attributed to their lengthy absences abroad — having built up a considerably reputation in such territories as Germany, Japan and America.

Connolly will remain with Polydor, and his solo career will be launched officially in the summer, by way of an album and single — with the likelihood of live appearances to follow.

— 20 —

Above: And then there were three – press coverage of Brian Connolly's departure in 1979. (*Michael Mandt*)

ブリティッシュ・ロック・シーンに一際光るヘヴィー・ハーモニー・ロックの雄

スイート来日。

ROCKUPATION SWEET

Left: August 1976 Japanese tour publicity – it would be 1978 before Sweet played live again. (*Michael Mandt*)

Below: Concert ticket from the 1978 *Level Headed* tour. (*Michael Mandt*)

Freitag, 3. Februar '78 · 19 Uhr
Ludwigshafen · Friedrich-Ebert-Halle
MAMA CONCERTS PRESENTS

LEVEL HEADED

SWEET

on Tour

VORVERKAUF: DM 16,–
zzgl. Vorverkaufsgebühr incl. MWSt.
ABENDKASSE: DM 18,–

Keine Haftung für Sach- und Körperschäden.
In keinem Falle Rückerstattungsanspruch
auf den Kaufpreis. · Vor Mißbrauch wird gewarnt.
Das Mitnehmen von Tonbandgeräten, Filmkameras
und Flaschen in die Halle ist grundsätzlich verboten!

№   3545

Kontroll-Abriß

Right: A Polydor publicity photo for the three-piece formation of the band, from 1979. (*Michael Mandt*)

SWEET

Above: Last man standing – Andy Scott on stage with Sweet, December 2019.
(*Eileen Handley*)

Head of BBC Radio, Ian Trethowan, rather backhandedly defended the record and the BBC's decision to play it, stating that youngsters, '…while possibly enjoying the easy beat of the music, will be unaffected by the words, since they are totally empty of real content – like all too much pop music.'

There was, however, still one major obstacle facing 'Teenage Rampage'. Mud, who had already enjoyed a no. 4 hit with that Chinn-Chapman song 'Dynamite', now found themselves pipping The Sweet for the top slot. Their song 'Tiger Feet' bagged the no. 1 position while 'Teenage Rampage' made it to no. 2. This clearly rankled with The Sweet and there were some frosty put-downs hurled in Mud's direction in the music press. It was a bit like a glam version of the 'Battle of Britpop' between Blur and Oasis in the mid-'90s, only with both bands sharing the same songwriting team and the same management. 'Frankly, we didn't think the Mud single would get to no. 1. The idea was that Sweet would get there first and, as that dropped, Mud would be coming up – With Suzi's record to follow that,' Chapman told *Disc* magazine. In hindsight, however, for all its nonsense lyrics and silly dance routines, 'Tiger Feet' was simply the better song.

The B-side of 'Teenage Rampage' was the band composition 'Own Up, Take A look At Yourself'. Although the track begins with some jingling sleigh bells, it is anything but a camp, seasonal ditty. Pounding riffs and Connolly furiously belting out lyrics about a wronged lover, it is yet another classic hard rock Sweet B-side.

In February 1974, The Sweet appeared in a BBC documentary *All That Glitters*. Aimed at a youth audience and screened in a late-afternoon slot, the film shows the band preparing for their Christmas 1973 *Top Of The Pops* appearance and also uses footage from the December 1973 Rainbow show. 'The Sweet appeals mainly to a young audience. Older people sometimes find their brand of showmanship and type of songs difficult to take,' intones narrator, Sarah Ward. 'We're gonna be around for ten years I think, as a group,' Scott tells the interviewer, somewhat prophetically (and luckily for this book!)

That same month also saw Connolly suffer a serious assault. Two assailants attacked him as he was leaving a pub in Staines, Middlesex, near his home. Left unconscious, he was found to have severe bruising to his throat. Not only did it affect the band's live schedule for 1974 and delay completion of the impending album it appears that the longer-term consequences may have been far more profound. 'I've never heard a range drop as drastically,' Scott told *Classic Rock* magazine in 2017. 'There was no way he could get anywhere near 'Set Me Free' when we began to tour America.'

Album Release
Sweet Fanny Adams

Personnel:

Brian Connolly: lead vocals, handclap and tambourine (except tracks 3, 7 and 8)

Steve Priest: bass guitar, six string bass, lead vocals (tracks 3 and 7), backing vocals

Andy Scott: guitars, lead vocals (track 8), backing vocals

Mick Tucker: drums, timpani, tubular bells, gong, voice effects, backing vocals

Produced at: Audio International Studios, London and Advision Studios, London, late 1973 to early 1974 by Phil Wainman.

UK release date: April 1974

Highest chart places: UK: 27, Germany: 2 US: Not released

Running time: 39:37

Recorded during sessions throughout late 1973 and early 1974, Sweet's second bona fide studio album and their first genuine rock album was finally released in April 1974. It was produced, once again, by Wainman. In spite of Chinn and Chapman providing two of the songs, both writers were committed overseas for much of the recording and neither were particularly involved, very much leaving the band and Wainman to set the direction.

Perhaps taking their escape from the saccharine world of bubblegum just a little too far, Tucker revealed that the band's original choice of title was somewhat more graphic than what finally materialised. 'We always wanted to call it Sweet Fuck All... but the record company wouldn't let us, so the next thing was to call it *Sweet Fanny Adams* but RCA compromised with us and let us use the song title 'Sweet F. A.'' Both phrases remain popular euphemisms to this day. The origins are considerably darker, however. Causing sensational headlines at the time and deep shock and revulsion throughout the country, 'Sweet' Fanny Adams was actually an eight-year-old girl who was brutally murdered by an abductor back in 1867.

The cover of the album showed the four members all glammed up in their shiny metallic stage-wear but with their rippled reflections beneath on a water-type effect, the aim being to show the murkier, more debauched, more rock and roll side of the band, according to Tucker. This was also the first release to drop the definite article from the band's name. From now on, all releases would be credited to Sweet, rather than The Sweet.

For all of the band's confidence about entering a new phase of their career, however, Connolly's devastating injuries delayed the completion of the album. Tucker discussed this in *The Sweet: No Matter What They Say* by Mick Duthie, published in 2018): 'It left Phil with half an album unfinished and we had to get injections for Brian to bring his voice back for eight hours at a time, but doing that would take two weeks off the healing period. And we just about got the album completed.'

'He (Brian) managed to get through the majority, but when it came to 'Restless' and 'No You Don't', it was hopeless,' Priest recalled in his autobiography. 'I was put forward as the candidate to sing the remaining songs, which were too high for me as well. After playing around with the tape speeds, I managed to finish the album with my own throat very sore.'

Technical and logistical problems aside, what was finally released comes out as an extraordinarily strong album indeed. When a remastered CD version of *Sweet Fanny Adams* was reissued in 2004, Scott wrote in the liner notes, 'This is the band at its finest – full of energy, humour and social statement of the era.'

'Set Me Free' (Scott)

The album opens with Scott's 'Set Me Free'. It was one of the songs that originated from demos that he had worked up alone the previous summer. 'Gagged, ball and chained; Feel just the same' the song begins with sexually charged lyrics. Yet 'Set Me Free' could also be interpreted as a manifesto for a band casting away the constraints imposed by external song-writers-cum-management and chart single success. And what a manifesto it is. Powerhouse drumming, thumping bass, searing guitar and those sumptuous vocal harmonies 'Set Me Free' is Sweet at their finest. Scott's original demo can be found on the 2017 box set reissue of the album. In later years, the song has been covered by Saxon, Motley Crue's Vince Neil, and Billy Idol's sidekick, Steve Stevens.

'Heartbreak Today' (Connolly / Priest / Scott / Tucker)

Initially written as something called 'We're Revolting', this underwent quite substantial revision before emerging as 'Heartbreak Today'. RCA were reportedly so impressed with this track that there was talk of releasing it as a single. With its chugging heavy riff, superb lead guitar from Scott, powerful melodic-yet-aggressive vocals from Connolly and layered harmony vocals from the rest, 'Heartbreak Today' is certainly something of a hard rock masterpiece. After a dramatic climax at over four minutes in, the track noodles along rather pointlessly for a little longer than necessary, but the momentum soon picks up again once the band power into the next song.

'No You Don't' (Chapman / Chinn)

'No You Don't' is one of only two Chinn-Chapman songs on the album and sees the songwriting duo move far away from the bubblegum/glam formula. Arguably, the track sounds more like a Chinn-Chapman attempt at writing a Connolly-Priest-Scott-Tucker B-side. Regardless, the band pull it off magnificently. Powerful and furious, one US reviewer deemed it, 'the most blatant Who rip-off in recent memory' but nevertheless lauded its musical ambition and the 'vicious conviction' with which Connolly blasts out the lyrics. It is actually Priest singing lead vocals on this one, however, with the bass player doing his very best Brian Connolly impersonation. Pat Benatar would later cover the song on her 1979 *In The Heat Of The Night* album.

'Rebel Rouser' (Connolly / Priest / Scott / Tucker)

If the previous track was about Chinn-Chapman writing a Connolly-Priest-Scott-Tucker song, then surely 'Rebel Rouser' is about Connolly-Priest-Scott-Tucker writing a Chinn-Chapman song! With a recycling of Eddie Cochran's 'Something Else' riff, 'Rebel Rouser' was described by one critic as the 'reincarnation of 'Hellraiser'' and put on the album 'just to prove to themselves that they could write their own Chinn-Chapman song.' With its knowing nods to rock and roll heritage, its thunderous drum work-out, catchy choruses and camp one-liners from Priest, the evidence is that the four could actually make a pretty good fist of doing just that.

'Peppermint Twist' (Dee / Glover)

Retrieved from the aborted *History of Rock* album, 'Peppermint Twist' is the one track that sticks out like a sore thumb on *Sweet Fanny Adams*. Originally recorded by Joey Dee & The Starlighters during the twist craze of the early 1960s, Sweet's campy, tongue-in-cheek, high-energy version is a fun, energetic cover in its own right and even became a surprise Australian no. 1 for the band when it was released there as a single. The Sweet's debut album would have been improved immensely had something like this been included rather than those insipid cabaret covers. But on *Sweet Fanny Adams*? At a time when the band were at pains to exhibit their credentials as a harder-edged rock act, it is the equivalent of trying to stick 'Twist and Shout' on the *Sergeant Pepper* album. 'We had only included it on the album as a joke because we had run out of songs and were three minutes short,' Priest later recalled.

'Sweet F. A.' (Connolly / Priest / Scott / Tucker)
Opening side two of the original vinyl release was the thunderous quasi-title track 'Sweet F. A.' Another hard rocker with shades of Led Zeppelin and Deep Purple, the ugly, violent nature of some of the lyrics ('if she don't spread, I'm gonna bust her head') make for uncomfortable listening in the modern age. The chorus, however, reads like another manifesto declaration from a band shaking off its bubblegum past and setting out its stall with righteous fury:

> Sweet F. A. never gonna make it
> Sweet F. A. people think we fake it
> Sweet F. A., now we're gonna take it

Coming in at over six minutes, fortunately the words are few, and the final two minutes comprise a spectacularly cacophonic heavy metal workout between Scott, Priest and Tucker, ending with a 'Hell Raiser'-style explosion. A classic slice of hard rock with the glorious, uncompromising sound of Sweet in full throttle, it remains a fan favourite to this day and is still a staple of the live set-list from Scott and co. It is best just not to dwell too much on some of the god-awful lyrics.

'Restless' (Connolly / Priest / Scott / Tucker)
With its chugging riff and some groovy bass, 'Restless' is the other track on the album where Priest sings lead – and a magnificent job he does of it too, regardless of the strain he said it put on his own vocal cords having to step in for Connolly.

'Into The Night' (Scott)
'Into The Night' is the third track on the album on which Connolly does not sing lead vocals. Fittingly, the vocals are handled by Scott as he alone gets the writing credit for this one. It was another of the songs that he

had worked up alone the previous summer and the original demo can be found on the CD re-release for the 2017 box set. Some nifty signature drum work from Tucker opens the track, and he also provides additional percussive effects in the instrumental break – with the gongs and bells and slowed-down voices giving the track a progressive, strangely experimental feel. This is one of the tracks that would be lifted from *Sweet Fanny Adams* for the US version of *Desolation Boulevard*.

'AC-DC' (Chapman / Chinn)

The second of the two Chinn-Chapman compositions on *Sweet Fanny Adams*. Combining risqué lyrics and hard rock riffs it is not about the Aussie rockers who were just starting up around that time but, rather, it is a tale of a bisexual female lover. Although the lyrics read more like a heterosexual male porn-star fantasy version of lesbianism rather than any sort of gay liberation anthem, it is nevertheless a great hard rock song – a classic slice of Sweet and a worthy conclusion to the album.

While the *NME* stayed firmly in the anti-Sweet camp, the album picked up favourable reviews from the likes of *Sounds*, *Record Mirror* and *Disc*, the latter stating, 'They've made an album far, far better than I, for one, would ever have believed them capable.' Although *Sweet Fanny Adams* was not released in the US, *Phonograph Record* magazine was clearly keeping a keen eye on what was happening in the UK. Reviewer, Ron Ross, praised the hook-laden, glam metal tracks like 'Rebel Rouser' and 'AC-DC' but was far more dismissive of songs like 'Sweet F. A.' and 'Restless'. Gary Sperrazza for the *Shakin' Street Gazette* argued: '*Sweet Fanny Adams* just gives them a chance to stretch out, without losing the essence of what makes them so good in the first place.'

Sweet Fanny Adams sold strongly in continental Europe, reaching no. 2 in Germany and no. 4 in Sweden, but only reached a highly respectable but nowhere near chart-topping no. 27 in the UK charts. Connolly's injuries meant that the band were unable to tour to promote it and *Sweet Fanny Adams* dipped out of the UK charts after just two weeks. The first Sweet album to chart, even counting the various compilations that had been released prior to this, it would be another 22 years (with the release of the *Ballroom Hitz* compilation in 1996) before a Sweet album would trouble the UK Top 40 again.

Though one could easily envisage, with the right promotion, *Sweet Fanny Adams* being absolutely ripe for the US market at the time, it never even got an official release in the States. Some of the tracks were cobbled together with some recent singles and some of the tracks from the subsequent *Desolation Boulevard* album to create the US version of *Desolation Boulevard* but Americans were to be denied the full, original, powerful impact of the *Sweet Fanny Adams* album until many years later.

As well as being unable to tour to promote the album, one hugely unfortunate consequence of Connolly's injuries was that the band had to turn down an invitation from The Who to support them at an open-air festival at Charlton Athletic football ground in south-east London. Attended by 50,000 rock fans, and with the likes of Bad Company, Humble Pie and Lou Reed on the bill, it would have been the perfect showcase for Sweet's transition from glam rock singles act to hard rock albums act. It was Sweet's appalling bad luck that they had to say no.

As well as the tensions between band and producer and band and songwriting team, 1974 had also witnessed growing tensions between Wainman and Chinn-Chapman, particularly Chapman, who, as the principal songwriter in the partnership, had clear ideas about how those songs should be produced. Wainman eventually ended the relationship and went off to work for acts like The Bay City Rollers and (after they had severed their own relationship with Chinn and Chapman) Mud. A new set-up was in place for the band's next single, albeit a relatively short-lived one.

Single Release
'The Six Teens' (Chapman / Chinn) b/w **'Burn On The Flame'** (Connolly / Priest / Scott / Tucker)

Personnel:

Brian Connolly: lead vocals

Steve Priest: bass guitar, backing vocals

Andy Scott: guitar, backing vocals

Mick Tucker: drums, backing vocals

Produced at Audio International Studios, London, May 1974 by Mike Chapman (production credit: Mike Chapman, Nicky Chinn and Phil Wainman)

UK release date: July 1974

Highest chart places: UK: 9, Germany: 4, US: Did not chart

After the over-the-top glam bombast of 'Teenage Rampage' despite the superficial similarities in song titles, Sweet's next single marked a significant change in direction. Musically, it has none of the obvious hallmarks of a typical early 1970s glam rock song and, visually, in their promotional appearances, the band are to be found in a more traditional hard rock uniform of jeans, T. shirts and leather rather than glitter and lurex. Telling the story of three teenage couples from the late 1960s to the (then) present day, it shows a far more mature approach, lyrically, than previous singles and alternates between lighter acoustic-based verses and riff-heavy choruses. Even the *NME*, who had been waging war on Sweet throughout the glam phase, gave it a favourable review. Hailed by both Connolly and Scott as Chinn-Chapman's finest work for the band, 'The Six Teens' is a fabulous, catchy, commercial, melodic hard rock song. It cannot really be regarded as glam rock. Aping *Sweet Fanny Adams*, it was also the first single to drop the definite article in the band's name and is credited to simply 'Sweet'. Their first hit without Wainman's involvement, production is actually credited to Chapman, Chinn and Wainman. However, Wainman later confirmed that this was more about tying up business loose ends than anything practical and that it was Chapman, alone, who produced the single. It reached no. 9 in the UK chart and secured a top 10 placing across much of Europe.

Always one of Connolly's favourite Sweet songs, it provided the soundtrack to an especially poignant moment at his funeral twenty-three years later as pall-bearers carried his coffin out of the church to the song at the end of the service.

The B-side is another catchy, commercially-sounding hard rock tune, the band-penned 'Burn On The Flame'. It complements Chinn and Chapman's own song, 'The Six Teens' perfectly. Indeed, this is probably the first case of the B-side of a Sweet single sounding 100% like the same musical genre as the A-side since their very first singles of the late 1960s.

Single Release
'Turn It Down' (Chapman / Chinn) b/w **'Someone Else Will'** (Connolly / Priest / Scott / Tucker)
Personnel:
Brian Connolly: lead vocals
Steve Priest: bass guitar, backing vocals
Andy Scott: guitar, backing vocals
Mick Tucker: drums, backing vocals
Produced at Audio International Studios, London, September 1974 by Mike Chapman in association with Nicky Chinn
UK release date: November 1974

Highest chart places: UK: 41, Germany: 4, US: Not released

Although a decision was taken not to include any singles on the *Sweet Fanny Adams* album and thus let the album stand or fall on its own merit, the second Sweet album of 1974 would include not just 'The Six Teens' but a second single, too. Released slightly ahead of *Desolation Boulevard*, if the aim was to secure another big hit to help publicise the album, then 'Turn It Down' failed spectacularly. The heaviest, rawest and least commercial-sounding Sweet single to date, it ran into problems with the BBC early on who objected to the (nowadays unbelievably innocuous) line 'for God's sake turn it down'. The BBC promptly banned the single from their playlists. Although it did better in continental Europe, without airplay, it struggled to a lowly no. 41 in the UK charts. My view, however, is that brilliant though it is as an album track, as a single, it is so raw-sounding compared to its predecessors that it was simply not commercial enough for the British charts and even with airplay, it could have struggled to have made the top 10. It was to be the last single penned by Chinn and Chapman that the band would release.

The B-side 'Someone Else Will' was a slightly cleaned-up version of the reworking of 'Burning' that the band had been using in their stage shows, with all the references to fucking now changed to oral sex: 'If we don't go down on you then someone else will'. Rock and roll!

Album Release
Desolation Boulevard

Personnel:
Brian Connolly: lead vocals (except track 5)
Steve Priest: bass, backing vocals, lead vocals
Andy Scott: guitars, synthesisers, backing vocals, lead vocals (track 5)
Mick Tucker – drums, percussion, backing vocals, arrangement (track 6)
Produced at Audio International Studios, London, September 1974 by Mike Chapman in association with Nicky Chinn
UK release date: November 1974
Highest chart places: UK: Did not chart, Germany: 9, US: 25 (different US version)
Running time: 39:54

For *Desolation Boulevard*, Wainman was gone and Chapman alone produced the album. In contrast to the highly-polished studio wizardry of *Sweet Fanny Adams*, a decision was taken to opt for a far looser quasi-live feel. 'I've seen you play live so often and I want to capture some of how good that is,' Chapman told the band at the time. Its iconic sleeve was designed by Hipgnosis and featured the four band members superimposed over a stylised image of California's Sunset Boulevard. The background photo was shot near the entrance of a rock music club called the Central, located at 8852 Sunset Boulevard in West Hollywood.

'The Six Teens' (Chapman / Chinn)
While the previous album steered away from singles. *Desolation Boulevard* proudly opens with the band's recent hit 'The Six Teens'. Not only that but even the album's title is culled from a line in the song: 'On Desolation Boulevard they'll light the faded light'. A more mature approach than we had witnessed with previous Chinn-Chapman hits and a perennial fan favourite, the dramatic but melancholic, bitter-sweet air of 'The Six Teens' fits in well with the spirit of the rest of the album, certainly in a way that 'Teenage Rampage', for example, would not have done by any stretch of the imagination.

'Solid Gold Brass' (Connolly / Priest / Scott / Tucker)
With a title and chorus inspired by the old phrase 'all that glistens is not gold' and the old cockney rhyming slang 'brass' (i.e., brass flute – prostitute), 'Solid Gold Brass' is a heavy, mid-paced rocker, with lyrics typical for hard rock outfits of the era. It has been compared to the likes of Aerosmith, and it is not difficult to see why later metal bands would be soaking up influences from tracks like this in later decades. Lead vocals are shared between Connolly and Priest, with Connolly singing the main chunk of each verse and Priest responding in a far more furious and far less camp reworking of the vocal interjections that had become a trademark on the band's earlier glam singles.

'Turn It Down' (Chapman / Chinn)
The second Chinn-Chapman song on *Desolation Boulevard*, Priest recalled that half-way through the recording of the album Chapman turned up with this as a brand-new song. It immediately met with Priest's approval: 'I liked it a lot, and we got exactly the right feel to it. It was the most enjoyable track I ever laid down with the band.' Tucker: 'He was trying to write as the Sweet would write, only in a commercial way. I mean he was bending over backwards to try and do that.' The brash and raucous 'Turn It Down' certainly makes for a great album track and one reviewer rightfully praised

Scott's 'loud and intentionally obnoxious guitar break'. One can easily see why it was a bit of a disaster as a single, however.

'Medusa' (Scott)

Placed one after the other at the end of the original side one, the album features two tracks written by Scott alone. The first of these is the proggy 'Medusa'. Inspired by the snake-haired gorgon of Greek-mythology who would turn onlookers into stone, it is a dramatic musical piece with classical influences, a slowed-down doom-laden instrumental break and a manic jazz–rock–influenced guitar solo. One of the band's most sophisticated tracks to date, it would not have been out of place on one of Uriah Heep's albums and it showed Sweet to be capable of singing about far more than simply ballrooms and wigwams. It remains one of the real highlights of the album.

'Lady Starlight' (Scott)

The second of the Scott compositions, the mellow, acoustic-based 'Lady Starlight' makes for something of a contrast to the rest of the album and is a nod to the melodic, soft-rock direction that the band would come to explore more fully on their 1978 album *Level Headed*. The track has been compared unfavourably to Bowie's 'Lady Stardust' from his 1972 *Ziggy Stardust* album, but beyond a similar title and similar tempo, there is not really much to compare the two. The track suitably impressed RCA that Scott was encouraged to rework the track for solo release the following year. Scott again on thesweetweb.com in 2018:

> When I wrote 'Lady Starlight' for inclusion in the album *Desolation Boulevard*, little did I realise that I would become the first member of Sweet to release a solo single. In fact, I didn't really imagine that I would even sing it; after all, Brian was the lead vocalist. Mike Chapman, our producer, immediately suggested that I sing the song after hearing a run-through in the studio with an acoustic guitar'. Once the album was completed, someone at RCA Records could see the potential of 'Starlight' as a single, but without Brian's voice, it was deemed a bit radical to put it out as a Sweet single, thus 'Lady Starlight' by Andy Scott was the answer.

'The Man With The Golden Arm' (Bernstein / Fine)

The original side two opens with an ambitious eight-and-a-half-minute long cover of 'The Man With The Golden Arm' based on Elmer Bernstein's film score from the 1955 Hollywood blockbuster of the same name. Aiming to capture some of the brassy pomp of the original and with a bevy of session players brought in for the occasion, the track's real purpose is to act as a showcase for Tucker's exceptional drumming skills. In the 1970s, drum solos were a de rigueur part of live performances in 'serious' rock circles. Very often, this led to the inclusion of the odd drum solo as part of a live disc, but as part of a studio recording, it was pretty unusual. Ambitious and impressive? Certainly. Whether an extended drum solo is something most listeners want to hear on a rock album, however – the jury is probably still out on that one.

'Fox On The Run' (Connolly / Priest / Scott / Tucker)

The next track on the album is the original version of 'Fox On The Run'. This was prior to it being completely revamped as a single some months later. Another group composition, it was still lacking a chorus before it could be committed to tape until Priest came up with an idea: 'As the song we were writing was about a groupie, maybe the word 'fox' should be incorporated.' The chorus and title were thus born. It was to be some months after the release of the album that the version that we are readily familiar with was to emerge. With none of the commerciality of the later re-recording and without the instantly-recognisable synthesiser intro and with a much rawer but far less catchy riff, it is interesting to see how this song evolved from the original album version. Only the style of vocal delivery remains largely unchanged across the two versions.

'Breakdown' (Connolly / Priest / Scott / Tucker)

Another group composition, 'Breakdown' is a simple, straight-ahead rocker. The penultimate track on the album, it is another superb showcase for Tucker's powerhouse drumming and those classic Sweet harmony vocals. The lyrics deal with the theme of failed relationships, disappointment and mental breakdown.

'My Generation' (Townshend)

With echoes of the tributes to Townshend et al. that featured in some of the band's early BBC sessions and still a staple of the live set at the time, the final track is a cover of The Who's 'My Generation'. 'We even asked Pete Townshend to guest on it, and he agreed,' recalled Priest. 'At the last minute, however, he declined. I think this may have been because we hadn't played at the Charlton gig.' However, by then, the band were so excited at the prospect of recording it, Connolly told one interviewer that they went ahead anyway. A faithful cover of the original, even down to the stuttering, and a call and response type vocal rather than the more lavish multi-layered trademark Sweet harmonies, it is debatable whether it really brings anything new to the table. Still, it consolidates the band's hard rock credentials, celebrates their musical heroes and is a wonderfully energetic conclusion to the album.

Although these days, the album is frequently lauded as the absolute 'must-have' if you are to only own one Sweet studio album, many of the reviews at the time were surprisingly lukewarm. Tucker's extended drum solo failed to find much favour with reviewers, and while there were some positive comments in the likes of *Sounds*, the reviews overall did not exactly set the world alight in terms of announcing to the world that here was a band confidently setting out in a new direction now glam's allure began to pale. Although the album sold in mainland Europe, it failed to make the charts at all in the UK.

A quite different version of *Desolation Boulevard* was released by Capitol the following year for the US market (with tracks culled from a mixture of the UK version of the album along with the previous *Sweet Fanny Adams* album, in addition to the 'Ballroom Blitz' and 'Fox On The Run' singles).

Unlike the relentless touring of previous years, a combination of Connolly's injuries and taking time in the studio to record two albums meant that Sweet only played 35 live gigs throughout 1974. There were a handful of UK gigs in late August, a European tour during October and a short UK tour across November and December. As part of the band's transition from teenybop act to hard rock outfit, the latter tour included a number of universities alongside the more usual ballrooms.

Just like the bubblegum to glam transition two years previously, 1974 had been a year of great change for Sweet. They had started the year as the archetypal glam rock singles act with an archetypal glam rock single and ended the year having released two hard rock albums of mainly self-penned material. Not only had they lost the definite article from the front of their name, they had also lost one-third of the Chinn-Chapman-Wainman triumvirate who had overseen their rise to fame and were about to lose the remaining two-thirds. 1975 would be another year of significant change for the band.

Chapter Seven: 1975 – Going It Alone

By 1975, glam had faded almost as rapidly as it appeared. Even by 1973-74, T. Rex singles were failing to make the top ten. By the middle of 1975, Bolan was by now struggling to make the top 20. Slade had seen the writing on the wall for glam, too, not only ditching Dave Hill's silver platforms and Noddy Holder's mirrored top hat but also exploring new musical pastures, with their bitter-sweet single 'How Does It Feel' and dark, gritty film *Flame* providing a marked change in direction for the band. Bowie had long since retired his Ziggy alter-ego and re-invented himself as a blue-eyed soul boy, enjoying a hit on both sides of the Atlantic with 'Young Americans'. Following the disappointing sales of *Desolation Boulevard* Sweet needed a new single that was appropriate for new times.

'Turn it Down' had demonstrated that while Chinn-Chapman could write great songs, some of these were actually better suited as album material rather than as singles. The same mistake was about to be made again. Another Chinn-Chapman song 'I Wanna Be Committed' was recorded as the band's next single but, thankfully, wiser heads prevailed. A superb and hard-hitting track for an album, it eventually wound up on the US version of *Desolation Boulevard* as well as the 1975 UK compilation *Strung Up*. Single material it was not, however. With Chinn-Chapman otherwise engaged and unable or unwilling to provide any further new songs, RCA suggested that the band revisit a handful of tracks from the recent *Desolation Boulevard* album and rework them as potential singles.

Single Release
'Fox On The Run' (Connolly / Priest / Scott / Tucker) b/w **'Miss Demeanour'** (Connolly / Priest / Scott / Tucker)
Personnel:
Brian Connolly: lead vocals
Steve Priest: bass guitar, backing vocals
Andy Scott: guitar, synthesiser, keyboards, backing vocals
Mick Tucker: drums, backing vocals
Produced at Kingsway Recorders Studio, London, January 1975 by Sweet
UK release date: March 1975
Highest chart places: UK: 2, Germany: 1, US: 5

Responding to RCA's suggestion, Priest maintained that there was no need to record more than one track and that they should simply concentrate on reworking 'Fox On The Run'. In mid-January 1975, for the first time but certainly not the last, the band booked themselves into Kingsway Recorders studio in London's Holborn. In this studio complex, recently taken over by Ian Gillan, the band set themselves up to record a brand-new version of 'Fox On The Run'. Not only was this to be the first single they had written themselves, but they would also be producing themselves, too, with the studio's co-owner, Louis Austin, as engineer.

With a manically-chirping synthesiser leading to a majestic keyboard intro, echo effects added to Connolly's powerful vocal, pitch-perfect harmonies and a gorgeous guitar solo from Scott, a great hard rock album track had been transformed into an exquisite single – every bit as iconic and memorable as the 'Blockbuster!'/'Hell Raiser'/'Ballroom Blitz' triumvirate from 1973. The record-buying public thought so, too. Scott: 'It was probably our attempt at being David Bowie … It had all those nuances in there. I just grabbed my hands on a pile of synthesisers and I wanted to experiment.'

A no. 2 hit in the UK and top five across much of the world, had Sweet done the unthinkable and not only moved from bubblegum to glam rock but then, just as glam was fading, ditched their songwriting team and chalked up a self-composed worldwide smash where they could finally be taken seriously as a credible rock act? Time would tell.

Priest recalled in his autobiography *Are You Ready Steve?* a conversation with Chapman at the time: 'I remember one Wednesday morning, the phone ringing in my little house in Hayes and hearing Mike Chapman on the other end. 'Well, I guess you won't be needing us anymore,' he said. I thought for about a nanosecond and replied, 'It doesn't look much like it, does it?' That was the end of that.'

Chinn: 'At the time, we were very upset, especially because the way we learned about their decision did not occur in a very direct way. There are no bad feelings now, but at that time, Mike and I were in America over Christmas having a vacation, and we got back to England to discover that they'd made 'Fox On The Run' themselves, which turned out to be a hit, so good for them, but somehow we felt that wasn't quite the way to do it.'

In subsequent years 'Fox On The Run' has gone on to be covered by any number of rock acts, including Girlschool, former Kiss guitarist Ace Frehley and the Red Hot Chilli Peppers. It has also made an appearance in numerous films and continued to attract new fans. The inclusion of 'Fox On The Run' in the trailer for the second volume of *Guardians Of The Galaxy* led to the song reaching no. 1 in the iTunes Rock Chart in 2016.

The riff-heavy 'Miss Demeanor' on the B-side is a less polished and far rawer-sounding hard rock number of the type we heard on *Desolation Boulevard*. Featuring Priest rather than Connolly on lead vocals, it was a song that the bass player brought to the band, although Chapman is also rumoured to have had a hand in writing it. Following the convention that the band had adopted for all of their B-sides in the Chinn and Chapman days, however, it is credited as a full band composition.

Although Sweet's touring schedule during the previous year had been greatly disrupted by Connolly's injuries, in the spring of 1975, they embarked on a nineteen-date tour across Denmark, Sweden and Germany during April and early May. In a review of one of the Swedish dates published in April 1975, even the *NME's* superior attitude to the band appeared to be thawing a little:

> In the past, I've probably been as guilty as anyone when it comes to sneering at chart-orientated groups. I wasn't exactly delighted at being asked to cover Sweet in Copenhagen but having done so I'm convinced that Sweet, and others like them, fill a need as relevant as that supposedly provided by artists like Rick Wakeman or ELP ... Sweet mix their hits liberally with tracks from *Sweet F. A.* and *Desolation Boulevard* and the audience enjoys it all. It's one thing to sing along with 'Hellraiser' and 'Blockbuster', quite another to enjoy cuts like 'Restless' or 'Set Me Free' that indicate Sweet really do rock as hard as anyone.

1975 would also see a switch of labels in the US, which would have important repercussions for the band's American market. Previous US releases had been on the Bell label and, as with a number of UK glam-era acts in the States, their impact on the US charts had been decidedly patchy. By signing a deal with Capitol, however, Sweet's management ensured the band were much better placed to begin making an impact commensurate with their aspirations as an albums-orientated rock act. The first release under the new Capitol deal was the US version of *Desolation Boulevard*. It plucked several tracks from the earlier *Sweet Fanny Adams* album and added some of the more recent singles alongside just two tracks from the actual UK version of *Desolation Boulevard* to create an album that was all Chinn and Chapman numbers on one side and band compositions on the other. In an interview with *Rolling Stone* in December 1975, Priest explained: 'Capitol picked the songs for the album. If we'd had our say, we'd have all our own tracks on it, obviously.'

The US version of *Desolation Boulevard* would peak at no. 25 in the Billboard album charts later that year and a re-release of the two-year-old 'Ballroom Blitz' single would also make the top five. Things were beginning to look promising for Sweet in the States, particularly in comparison to other UK acts like T. Rex and Slade. The band would make their live debut in the US later that year.

Single Release
'Action' (Connolly / Priest / Scott / Tucker) b/w **'Sweet F. A.'** (Connolly / Priest / Scott / Tucker)

Personnel:
Brian Connolly: lead vocals
Steve Priest: bass guitar, backing vocals
Andy Scott: guitar, synthesisers, backing vocals
Mick Tucker: drums, backing vocals
Produced at Audio International Studios, London, May 1975 by Sweet and Audio International Studios, London, 1974 by Phil Wainman
UK release date: July 1975
Highest chart places: UK: 15, Germany: 2, US: 20

The follow-up to 'Fox On The Run' was the song 'Action'. Although a remixed version of it eventually ended up on the following year's *Give Us A Wink* album, it was written and recorded separately from the rest of the album. Originally titled 'Piece of the Action', Priest recalled in his autobiography that it was written as a riposte to the business managers and record company executives (not to mention the taxman in the days when the top rate of income tax in the UK was 83%) who all seemed to be making money out of Sweet, but not much of it was filtering through to the band themselves. Priest: 'It seemed to me that everyone around us was getting rich and we were not.'

Connolly delivers his lines with righteous burning fury while the effects and arrangements (from the ker-ching of a cash register to the synthesiser intro, to the lush vocal overdubs, to the instrumental break) all serve to make 'Action' the most ambitious and sophisticated single Sweet had released to date. Scott: 'It's got all the ingredients of a rock band. You know – modulation, tempo changes, key changes, vocal gymnastics, riffs that are memorable. It's got everything – even backwards drums in the middle!' Indeed, over the years, numerous parallels have been drawn with Queen's 'Bohemian Rhapsody' which was released several months later. In later years, the song would be covered by New Wave Of British Heavy Metal outfit Raven, in 1981 and was also released as a single by Def Leppard in 1994; the latter's Joe Elliott has always been forthright about the influence of glam rock and Sweet on his own musical career.

For the B-side, there was no new track recorded. Rather, 'Sweet F. A.' was lifted from the previous year's *Sweet Fanny Adams* album. Of course, the band were no longer confined to B-sides to showcase their writing credentials, so there was less pressure to come up with something new and original as there was in the Chinn and Chapman days. Also, the lyrical themes dealt with in both 'Action' and 'Sweet F.A.' are not a million miles away from each other, so in that way, the decision kind of makes sense.

Although the single only made no. 15 in the UK charts, it did not appear to provoke a huge amount of soul-searching or existential fear within the band. Serious hard rock acts did not need to make the top five of the singles charts, of course, as long as they could sell albums. 'Singles aren't that important to us anymore. Albums are what we're concentrating on," Connolly told one interviewer. Whether they could sell those albums in any sizeable quantity, of course, would be the band's big test.

Sweet began recording songs for their next album in the summer of 1975 at Musicland Studios in Munich, with the final mixing and overdubs completed in London. Priest said in his autobiography that the decision to record in Germany was taken in an effort to reduce the band's tax liabilities. According to Priest, the sessions at Munich were also where cocaine began to get introduced into the band's routine. It did not appear to have had much negative impact on the recording of *Give Us A Wink,* but by the following album *Off The Record,* things would begin to get out of control.

Although recording for *Give Us A Wink* was completed in 1975, it would not go on sale until the following year. The US version of *Desolation Boulevard* had only just been released in the States and record company executives did not want to sap its potential by releasing a follow-up album too early. Delaying it would at least mean Sweet's US and European releases would be coterminous, but it did mean that there would be an awfully long gap in the European market before a new product arrived. RCA's solution was a compilation album.

Album release
Strung Up
Personnel:
Brian Connolly: lead vocals

Steve Priest: bass, backing vocals
Andy Scott: guitars, synthesisers, backing vocals
Mick Tucker: drums, backing vocals
Produced by Sweet, Mike Chapman, Nicky Chinn and Phil Wainman at various locations
UK release date: November 1975
Highest chart places: UK: Did not chart, Germany: 12, US: Not released
Running time: 74:15
Tracks listing:
Live album – disc one: 1. Hellraiser (Chapman / Chinn) 2. Burning / Someone Else Will (Connolly / Priest / Scott / Tucker) 3. Rock 'n' Roll Disgrace (Connolly / Priest / Scott / Tucker) 4. Need A Lot Of Lovin' (Connolly / Priest / Scott / Tucker) 5. Done Me Wrong Alright (Connolly / Priest / Scott / Tucker) 6. You're Not Wrong For Lovin' Me (Connolly / Priest / Scott / Tucker) 7. The Man With The Golden Arm (Bernstein / Fine)
Compilation album – disc two: 1. Action (Connolly / Priest / Scott / Tucker) 2. Fox On The Run (Connolly / Priest / Scott / Tucker) 3. Set Me Free (Scott) 4. Miss Demeanour (Connolly / Priest / Scott / Tucker) 5. Ballroom Blitz (Chapman / Chinn) 6. Burn On The Flame (Connolly / Priest / Scott / Tucker) 7. Solid Gold Brass (Connolly / Priest / Scott / Tucker) 8. The Six Teens (Chapman / Chinn) 9. I Wanna Be Committed (Chapman / Chinn) 10. Blockbuster! (Chapman / Chinn)

When another Sweet compilation was first mooted, RCA were initially considering a fairly standard mix of hit singles and B-sides. The band were able to persuade them to take a somewhat more imaginative approach, however. The resulting product was a double album that was part studio compilation and part live recording. The first disc brought together a mixture of A and B-sides, a couple of previously released album tracks and the hitherto unreleased 'I Wanna Be Committed' track, together with an alternate mix of the recent 'Action' single. The second disc, meanwhile, took seven tracks from the December 1973 Rainbow concert.

The entire Rainbow concert recording is reviewed in full in the chapter for 1973, while the previously released studio material is also reviewed in the relevant chapters. Although utilising the same studio recording, *Strung Up* does includes a unique mix of 'Action' that is different to both the single released earlier in the year and the version that would appear on the *Give Us A Wink* album the following year.

The only completely new studio track on *Strung Up*, however, is the band's recording of Chinn and Chapman's 'I Wanna Be Committed', which was laid down at the time of the sessions for the *Desolation*

Boulevard album. With stoner rock-esque lyrics about a man on the verge of insanity, this was the last ever song to be offered to Sweet by Chinn-Chapman as a potential single before the band cut loose and decided they could make it on their own. A good hard rock song, with its freaky distorted guitar, changes in tempo and studio sound effects trickery, the band make a very decent fist of it. However, as potential single material, it is fairly unremarkable, even if its lyrical content had succeeded in getting past the BBC censors. It certainly pales against both glam-era classics like 'Ballroom Blitz' or the post-glam singles like 'The Six Teens'. Moreover, it also reveals that, even as a potential album track, Sweet were actually writing far stronger songs of their own by this stage. There is nothing at all wrong with Sweet's delivery of 'I Wanna Be Committed', but it does demonstrate that band's decision to concentrate on their own material from now on was absolutely 100% the right one.

Bringing together previously released highlights from the band's more recent career and recordings from the incendiary live Rainbow concert was a bold attempt to do something a bit different than simply bang out another compilation. However, although the album is certainly more cohesive and more satisfying than, say, *The Sweet's Biggest Hits* released three years previously, the studio compilation still suffers somewhat from being neither quite one thing nor the other. It is neither a proper retrospective of the excellent, self-penned hard rock B-sides that the band had been putting out since they first signed with RCA, nor is it a comprehensive collection of their greatest hits.

In its gatefold sleeve, the album is more lavishly packaged than any previous Sweet compilation. The artwork is a symbolic representation of the band's newfound creative independence. The front cover shows stylised airbrushed drawings of the four band members apparently operating the strings at a Victorian puppet theatre. Once the gatefold sleeve is opened up and folded out, however, the back cover reveals that the four 'puppets' the band are operating are actually the four members of Sweet themselves, performing live on stage. Artist Joe Petagno would also go on to do the sleeve design for the following album. In an insert in the original pressings of the album, the record company seemingly expressed their immense pleasure at having Sweet on their books, stating: 'RCA take great pride in having played a part in their career and we look forward to a long and fruitful association.' The small print at the bottom of the insert explains there has been a cock-up on the track listing printed on the sleeve artwork – perhaps the main reason for the insert.

Despite RCA's declaration of pride and in spite of some reasonable reviews, as with previous Sweet compilations, it failed to make the UK charts. Indeed, it would be 1984 before any sort of Sweet compilation graced the British album charts – when the *Sweet 16* compilation finally scraped in at no. 49.

Following their European tour in the first half of the year, Sweet also embarked on a tour of New Zealand and Australia in the second half. Sweet were huge down-under and 'Peppermint Twist' was even a surprise no. 1 for the band in 1974, when RCA in Australia took it upon themselves to release a single from the *Sweet Fanny Adams* album. Beginning in Auckland, New Zealand, in August 1975, and taking in the likes of Wellington and Christchurch prior to moving on to a nine-date leg around Australia, the tour would conclude with two dates in the US, in Seattle and California. The Seattle date on 11 September would mark the band's live debut in the US. Now recognised internationally as the birthplace of grunge and responsible for the mega-rise of bands like Nirvana, it was a fairly inauspicious start for Sweet in the States back in 1975. In his autobiography, Priest recalls the venue being about half full, with around 650 people, but he contends that this was part of a strategy from their co-manager at the time, Ed Leffler, who was keen on a low-key start, via radio airplay and word of mouth, rather than lots of high-profile media appearances.

Compared to the difficult times that the band went through during the previous year, 1975 was an encouraging year for Sweet. Their first self-penned single had been a global smash, they were beginning to make a serious impact in terms of US sales and their transition from UK glam singles act to internationally-acclaimed album-oriented hard rock band appeared to be heading in the right direction.

Chapter Eight: 1976 – Give Us A Wink

1976 would be the year that Sweet not only released their first self-produced album with songs wholly composed by the band, it would also be the year that they put some serious effort into trying to crack America. Ever since the 'British invasion' of the mid-1960s, tapping into the US market had been held up as a kind of creative and commercial nirvana by many British bands. For some of the groups who had been part of the early 1970s British glam rock movement, cracking that market would continue to remain somewhat elusive. Over in the Slade camp, for example, by the mid-1970s making a US breakthrough was the band's number one goal. According to biographer, Chris Charlesworth, it had become 'virtually an obsession for them', with a band relocation to the States and near-constant touring. Even with that amount of effort, however, Slade failed to have even one single or album reach the US top 50 until well into the early 1980s. In terms of record sales, by the start of 1976, Sweet had already enjoyed significantly more success than Slade and, following their two debut US gigs the previous Autumn, now was the year to begin consolidating that with some serious touring as well as a new uncompromising hard rock album. The band would tour the States throughout late January, February and March. First, however, they would start the year with the release of a new single.

Single Release
'The Lies In Your Eyes' (Connolly / Priest / Scott / Tucker) b/w
'Cockroach' (Connolly / Priest / Scott / Tucker)
Personnel:
Brian Connolly: lead vocals
Steve Priest: bass guitar, backing vocals
Andy Scott: guitar, synthesizer, backing vocals
Mick Tucker: drums, backing vocals
Produced at AIR Studios, London and Musicland Studios, Munich, 1975 by Sweet
UK release date: January 1976
Highest chart places: UK: 35, Germany: 5, US: not released

'The Lies In Your Eyes' was lifted from the forthcoming *Give Us A Wink* and released as a single a few weeks prior to the launch of the album, along with another track, 'Cockroach', on the flip-side. Although it secured a top ten placing in several countries, it only reached a relatively lowly no. 35 in the UK charts. Both tracks are considered in full as part of the album review below.

The band appeared fairly ambivalent about UK hit singles at this stage, however. 'We were basically telling Britain to fuck off,' Connolly later admitted. 'Everything we did from then on was geared completely towards America.' The band thus headed out to commence their US tour, starting at the Memorial Auditorium in Chattanooga, Tennessee, on 21 January 1976. Not for them the grind of support slots, Sweet launched straight into a headlining tour with support provided by US singer-songwriter Eric Carmen, who had enjoyed a big hit with 'All By Myself'. Fellow Brit rockers, Status Quo, who were equally hungry for that US breakthrough, had initially been approached to provide support for Sweet but declined.

Although the *Give Us A Wink* album would be due out in a matter of weeks, the band had taken the decision to build this tour around older material that fans would already have some familiarity with, rather than use it to promote the new album. The set-list leant heavily on the US version of *Desolation Boulevard* (compiled from tracks off the British releases of *Boulevard* and its predecessor *Sweet Fanny Adams*) and featured songs like 'Ballroom Blitz', 'The Six Teens', 'No You Don't' 'AC-DC' and 'Set Me Free'. Tucker's drum solo showcase 'The Man With The Golden Arm' also featured, again making use of film clips with the drummer playing alongside himself in real-time.

A review in *Scene* magazine for the 26 February gig in Ohio highlighted the band's stage-craft and experience, gained from relentless touring since the early teenybop days, and praised Scott's guitar technique: 'Andy Scott's jazz-like solo runs in 'Restless' revealed a guitarist with influences other than Pete Townshend and Ritchie Blackmore, and the structure of their songs rests a notch or two above the average in complexity.'

The tour was an ambitious one, crisscrossing the States as a headlining act and eschewing the smaller venues to perform at places with capacities of several thousand. Although some dates were a sell-out, in cities where the band were less well-known, the venues were far from full. A climactic end to the tour, however, came in Santa Monica on 24 March, where the band were joined on stage by none other than Ritchie Blackmore. Priest: 'We were supposed to have been supported by a band called Back Street Crawler. Tragically, however, the night before the gig, Paul Kossoff, who was previously the guitarist with Free, took one Quaalude too many and died … A major event of that night was when Ritchie Blackmore played 'All Right Now' with us as a tribute to Paul.'

After a few weeks break on returning to the UK, rehearsals then began for a further European tour, beginning on 30 April and proceeding throughout the first half of May with gigs in Denmark, Sweden and Germany. Unlike the US tour, however, the European tour was aimed squarely at promoting the brand-new album, which had been released in February.

Album Release
Give Us A Wink
Personnel:
Brian Connolly: lead vocals, string machine
Steve Priest: bass guitar, vocals, celli
Andy Scott: guitars, vocals, celli, synthesisers, voice bag
Mick Tucker: percussion, vocals, celli, phased gong
Trevor Griffin: piano solo (track 4)
Produced at Musicland Studios, Munich; AIR Studios, London; Audio International Studios and Kingsway Recorders, London, 1975 by Sweet
UK release date: February 1976
Highest chart places: UK: Did not chart, Germany: 9, US: 27
Running time: 38:14

Probably the heaviest of Sweet's 1970s albums and the first to contain entirely band-written compositions, *Give Us A Wink* was also the first Sweet album to be self-produced. It was recorded mainly in Munich's Musicland studios the previous year. The studios had been established by Italian record producer and songwriter Giorgio Moroder in the late 1960s. By the 1970s, they had become a favoured destination for numerous English rock bands, including Led Zeppelin and the Rolling Stones, many of whom had been encouraged by managers and accountants to record albums abroad for tax purposes. Sweet were no different in this regard, with the bulk of the album being made in Munich over the summer of 1975. Overdubs and final mixing was then undertaken at Kingsway Recorders in London, together with an additional session at AIR to lay down the new single 'The Lies In Your Eyes'. Although everything was recorded and all wrapped up, ready for release in late 1975, the launch of the album was held back until February 1976 so as to ensure simultaneous release dates for both the European and American markets. Although not always afforded the same status as *Sweet Fanny Adams* or *Desolation Boulevard*, *Give Us A Wink* nevertheless remains one of the high points of Sweet's career, an album of searing, melodic, hard rock perfection.

The graffiti-strewn, cut-out cover, once again by American artist Joe Petagno, depicts a pair of eyes superimposed over a brick wall, with the cut-out allowing the left eye to wink by virtue of pulling the illustrated inner sleeve up and down. The title, a play on the very British slang word for masturbation (recalling a phrase that Connolly had been known to enjoy using on stage), probably left US audiences completely baffled. The cover was certainly eye-catching, though, even if the double-entendre passed many non-British audiences by.

'The Lies In Your Eyes' (Connolly / Priest / Scott / Tucker)

Unlike the majority of the album, which was recorded in Munich, this track was recorded entirely in London, at AIR Studios, with the specific intention of creating a follow-up single to 'Action'. With the synthesisers that had been deployed so effectively on recent singles, once again, supplementing the band's guitar-based hard rock and harmony vocals, some have sought to dismiss this as a poor man's 'Fox On The Run'. That is unfair. Although it had only a modest impact on the charts when released as a single, it, nevertheless, immediately sets the tone for the album as a whole: melodic, well-crafted, well-produced, polished yet accessible hard rock. A thumping rhythm from Tucker, powerful vocals from Connolly and some Stonesy-type riffing from Scott in places, alongside that embrace of, for then, state of the art studio technology makes this a powerful album opener. Indeed, The *Sounds* review of the album specifically mentions this track, accusing the band of taking the synthesiser intro from The Who and nicking the bass-line from The Stones but managing to come up with something that is totally Sweet. Even *Sounds* had to concede: 'That's class.' As a single, the song was never going to be as memorable as, say, 'Fox On The Run' or 'Action', but here it more than stands up against the likes of 'Sweet F. A.' or 'Solid Gold Brass' or any number of killer hard rock tracks Sweet had delighted us with on their two previous albums.

'Cockroach' (Connolly / Priest / Scott / Tucker)

The track was apparently named after an encounter Connolly had with a woman in Munich who 'crawled in the bed like a cockroach'. When the singer subsequently relayed the experience to Priest, it inspired the latter to come up with the song title. One of the hardest and least commercial tracks on the album, it opens with a Bonham-esque drum break from Tucker, soon to be followed by some heavy riffing from Scott and vocals delivered with absolute fury by Connolly. As with 'The Lies In Your Eyes', this track also had an early outing a few weeks prior to the release of the album as the single's B-side. A demo version of 'Cockroach' was released in the 1990s on the *Platinum Rare* album, and in the sleeve notes, Scott praises the sound for being 'much bigger' than the released version 'and to some extent better'. It is still an enormously powerful track in either format.

'Keep It In' (Connolly / Priest / Scott / Tucker)

While any rumours that Led Zeppelin's John Paul Jones played on the album turned out to be false, the band did nevertheless receive a visit from him while recording this track in Munich. Beginning with the sound effect of a passing supersonic aircraft, it provides an apt metaphor for what is about to unfold. This is another track that sees Sweet rocking out as raw and as hard as they come, almost having the feel of a studio jam in places. The drumming on the track is so heavy and relentless it has been compared to one continuous drum solo. Scott and Priest, meanwhile, also compete for attention with heavy riffing on guitar and bass. The musical one-upmanship never quite gets in the way of the band still managing to deliver a fine song, with a clear melody and those sumptuous vocal harmonies.

'4th Of July' (Connolly / Priest / Scott / Tucker)

Clearly demonstrating Sweet's fascination for all things American by this stage and deliberately setting out to use phraseology that would instantly resonate with the US public, '4th Of July' is one of the definite high points of the album. With its anthemic chorus, relentless rhythm and classy synth, the track represents album-oriented post-glam Sweet at its finest. Unique to this track, there is also an extended avant-garde style piano solo from musician and Sweet roadie Trevor Griffin (who would go on to co-write 'Love Is Like Oxygen' two years later). His welcome contribution thus ensures something of a departure from the typical guitars/synths/drums template that has been established for the album as a whole. Again, an earlier version of this track was eventually released on the *Platinum Rare* album and, again, Scott appears to favour it over the released version: 'I think this shows how great the band sounds without masses of overdubs.' Both versions work, however. In some ways, it is understandable that with advances in studio technology, coupled with Sweet now being free to make their own creative decisions that they would want to experiment a little. The only real curiosity is why it was never chosen as a single. With its embrace of American culture, it would have been perfect for the American audiences while providing British and European fans with a touch of faraway glamour.

'Action' (Connolly / Priest / Scott / Tucker)

The remixed version that appears on the album represented the third version of 'Action' to be released in the space of just seven months. Although not recorded along with the rest of the album and instead laid down as a standalone single at Audio International Studios some months earlier, it so perfectly fits the mood of the album that it would be inconceivable for it not to be a key track on *Give Us A Wink*. However, there was some debate in the Sweet camp about whether a reworked version of 'Action' should appear on the album or, indeed, whether it should be left off altogether. In the end, wiser heads prevailed and this remixed version is the version that appears on the album. The remix was undertaken by studio engineer Reinhold Mack in Munich, who was briefed to come up with something that sounded bigger. A little longer than the original, with an extended intro but without the trademark yell, it is a slightly more muscular mix. Whether a remix was entirely essential, however, is another matter entirely. A sign, perhaps, that far from being someone else's puppets, the band were now in danger of having more freedom than they could possibly know what to do with.

'Yesterday's Rain' (Connolly / Priest / Scott / Tucker)

The title for this track came from a line in a TV show, according to Priest in *The Sweet: No Matter What They Say*, where one of the characters was heard to say, 'I didn't come down with yesterday's rain'. Priest was inspired thus: 'I went, 'Fuck, that's a title if ever I heard one,' and it immediately became one.' A bluesy hard rocker with big, powerful riffs, equally big production and sexually explicit lyrics, Priest and co demonstrate that they can do far more than come up with catchy titles. The track adds to the overall heaviness of the album and remains one of the highlights.

'White Mice' (Connolly / Priest / Scott / Tucker)

Seemingly, a euphemism for ejaculation, Sweet give us yet more sexually charged and somewhat misogynistic lyrics when they up the pace once again with 'White Mice'. An out and out rocker with pulsating rhythms and heavy riffs, the falsetto harmonies provide a perfect foil for Connolly's furiously delivered lead vocal. Scott adds texture with some equally furious guitar soloing. 'White Mice' really has all the sonic ingredients you would expect from Sweet at the pinnacle of their hard rock phase.

'Healer' (Connolly / Priest / Scott / Tucker)

Opening with an explosive 4/4 backbeat from Tucker and a Led Zeppelin-type feel, 'Healer' was apparently inspired by an episode of *Star Trek*. Driven by Tucker's drumming and managing to be both hypnotic and anthemic at the same time, 'Healer' pounds away relentlessly for over seven minutes. It concludes the album in style and helps ensure *Give Us A Wink* easily stands up against anything being put out by the hard rock super-league groups around that time.

While the *Sounds* review threw around accusations that the album was derivative, it nevertheless gave a grudgingly enthusiastic three-star review and suggested that if readers were tired of waiting for the next Zeppelin, Who, or Stones album they may want to give *Give Us A Wink* a try. Other UK music papers were less enthusiastic. Over in the US, meanwhile, Richard Riegel for *Creem* magazine enthused: 'Get Sweet's *Give Us A Wink* now, and tune in to the best British Invasion since Slade hocked their spellers to buy guitars.'

Although the album made an impressive no. 27 in the US, it failed to chart at all in the UK. Not only were a number of other former glam acts, such as Slade, finding the transition to mainstream rock appeal equally difficult but, by 1976, a number of the hard rock album-oriented acts that had begun life at the turn of the decade themselves seemed to be giving the impression of running out of steam. Sweet's old friends Deep Purple called it a day in 1976. Uriah Heep fired their lead singer, David Byron, that same year amidst increasing problems with alcohol dependency. Similar issues were also occurring with Ozzy Osbourne in Black Sabbath, who quit the band temporarily in 1978 and then quit for good the following year. At the same time, 1976 saw punk beginning to take off as a musical subculture in the UK, the DIY ethos of the punks contrasting greatly to the somewhat bloated, cocaine-addled, millionaire lifestyle of many of the global rock supergroups. It would be a supreme irony for Sweet that just as they had finally thrown off the shackles of the manufactured pop world, they had first entered and immersed themselves fully into the business of hard rock respectability that they had so craved, that the genre, itself, was facing something of a crisis.

In this mid-1970s post-glam age, there was one band producing catchy, highly commercial, hard rock with lush vocal harmonies which were starting to do very well indeed: Queen. Queen were certainly glamorous, but they were never exactly glam. Although they began releasing albums in 1973, they only really began to reach stratospheric levels of success with their 'Bohemian Rhapsody' single, which spent nine weeks at the top of the UK charts following its release in 1975. Moreover, they had written their own songs from the outset and had neither the bubblegum tag nor the glam rock tag hanging around them in the way Sweet had. This was clearly beginning to rankle with Sweet. 'Queen are winkers', said one partially scrubbed-out piece of fake graffiti scrawled on the back of the *Give Us A Wink* album cover.

Preparations for a new album and a follow-up single to 'Lies In Your Eyes' began in the summer and the band originally booked themselves into Ramport Studios in south London, owned by The Who. The band demoed a couple of tracks here but found the experience to be an unsatisfactory one, expressing unhappiness not just with the studio but with the surrounding area and the lack of decent pubs. The sessions were soon abandoned. The band took off on another tour – this time to Japan – and recording eventually recommenced in September at Audio International Studio, where the band had recorded their *Desolation Boulevard* album and many of their glam hits.

The Japanese tour in August of that year saw the band perform nine dates, including four consecutive nights at the Nakano Sun Plaza in Tokyo, the same venue where Scorpions would record their celebrated *Tokyo Tapes* album two years later. The final Sun Plaza gig was committed to tape and initially surfaced as a bootleg prior to getting an official release in the early 1990s courtesy of two CDs, *Rock & Roll Disgrace* and *Land of Hope and Glory*. Although the audio quality leaves something to be desired, the recordings do provide a record of Sweet's stage show at the time, with 'You're Not Wrong for Loving Me' and 'Lady Starlight' providing lighter moments amongst the hard rock anthems and the Chinn-Chapman hits. The concert concludes with Scott's guitar blasting out Elgar's famous patriotic refrain in a style reminiscent of Jimi Hendrix's iconic feedback-laden rendition of 'The Star-Spangled Banner' at Woodstock. The tour concluded with a sell-out gig at the 7,000 capacity Budokan in Tokyo on

28 August 1976. It would be January 1978 before Sweet played another live gig again.

Single Release
'Lost Angels' (Connolly / Priest / Scott / Tucker) b/w 'Funk It Up' (Connolly / Priest / Scott / Tucker)
Personnel:
Brian Connolly: lead vocals
Steve Priest: bass guitar, backing vocals
Andy Scott: guitar, keyboards, synthesisers, backing vocals
Mick Tucker: drums, backing vocals
Produced at Audio International Studios, London, September 1976 by Sweet
UK release date: October 1976
Highest chart places: UK: Did not chart, Germany: 13, US: Not released

'Lost Angels' from the Audio International sessions was selected as the next single. After coming up with two unforgettable hard rock anthems in 'Fox On The Run' and 'Action', the follow-up, 'The Lies In Your Eyes' always sounded more like just another really great album track in comparison. Unfortunately, 'Lost Angels' compounds that problem. The track showcases slick production with hard-rocking riffs, melding with (for the time) state-of-the-art synth noodling, Connolly is in fine voice and Tucker his usual force of nature. It makes for a potent album track on *Off The Record* the following year. As a stand-alone-single, however, it lacks the killer hooks that would draw in more casual buyers alongside hardcore Sweet fans. At this point, Sweet were well past the stage where anything they put out would automatically enter the charts. The single failed to make the charts at all in the UK, the first single to not register a chart placing since 'Get On The Line' was released back in 1970. It did better elsewhere, particularly in the more loyal German and Scandinavian markets. It reached no. 5 in Sweden and no. 13 in Germany, for example, but in Australia struggled in at no. 74. Reviews saw inevitable comparisons with Queen, but while the combination of vocal harmonies, big production, hard rock riffage and studio wizardry was clearly working for Queen, Sweet did not have the same good fortune.

The B-side to 'Lost Angels' was 'Funk It Up', which was the band's first foray into the world of disco, a genre that was rapidly gaining popularity in the mid to late 1970s. 'I hated 'Funk It Up',' Connolly later confessed. 'But I knew why we recorded it and that was fine.' The track is skilfully executed and repurposes Sweet's trademark vocal harmonies and transplants them into a world of funk licks and disco beats alongside lyrics about shaking your head. Whether you enjoy listening to it or not is largely down to how much you like disco music. Personally, I agree with Connolly. I absolutely detest it. However, you have to give the band credit, at least on the innovation front. Rock stars making disco music was going to become a thing, but 'Funk It Up' was released some eighteen months before the Rolling Stones went down that route with 'Miss You' and some two years before Rod Stewart released 'Do Ya Think I'm Sexy'. Even those other 1960s veterans The Bee Gees had only released their first disco single that same summer. It was quite ironic that after beginning their hit singles career with the sound of the latest commercial pop trend on the A-sides and out-and-out hard rock on the B-sides, five years later, Sweet would end up putting out a single with hard rock on the A-side and the latest disco craze on the B-side. Released as a twelve-inch extended remix in the US the following year, 'Funk It Up' even became something of a cult hit on the US disco scene and reached no. 88 in the mainstream Billboard charts.

With no more touring, the latter part of 1976 was focused on recording and putting the finishing touches to the forthcoming *Off The Record* album. This was undertaken mainly at Audio International Studios before the band relocated, once again, to the familiar confines of Kingsway Recorders. With fewer chart successes the band were now less in demand for TV appearances. Slots on *Top of The Pops* were now a thing of the past, at least until 1978. However, the band did fly out to Germany that December to perform 'Lost Angels' on the *Musikladen* programme for their still appreciative German audience.

1976 had seen the band releasing their first self-produced, entirely self-written album. It was an album that would remain influential many years after it was recorded, while the subsequent single would point the way to a more polished, slightly more AOR approach on the next album. Problems were also on the horizon, though: declining record sales; a diminishing public profile which, even when they did get noticed, would often attract unfavourable comparisons with Queen; intra-band conflicts and spiralling cocaine use.

Chapter Nine: 1977 – Final Year At RCA

If 1976 had been the year that Sweet's ambitions of being a credible album-oriented rock act with a large and potentially lucrative fan-base in the United States were starting to bear fruit, 1977 would be the year that it started to unravel. 1977 would see disappointing sales for Sweet's latest album, flop singles, a cancelled US tour and growing tensions within the band. However, the year would also see a switch to a new record label and preparations for another new album that would herald a major change in direction.

Single Release
'Fever of Love' (Connolly / Priest / Scott / Tucker) b/w **'Distinct Lack of Ancient'** (Connolly / Priest / Scott / Tucker)
Personnel:
Brian Connolly: lead vocals
Steve Priest: bass guitar, backing vocals
Andy Scott: guitar, keyboards, synthesisers, backing vocals
Mick Tucker: drums, backing vocals
Produced at Kingsway Recorders, London, January 1977 by Sweet
UK release date: February 1977
Highest chart places: UK: Did not chart, Germany: 9, US: Not released

'Fever of Love' was the second single taken from the forthcoming *Off The Record* album. The band had originally flagged up another song from the album 'Live For Today' as the next single, but once 'Fever of Love' was written, it quickly became the favoured choice. With a driving riff, catchy chorus, a strong lead vocal from Connolly, some nice vocal interjections from Priest and, of course, those exquisite harmonies, 'Fever of Love' does sound more akin to hit single material than merely another great album track, even if it did not make much of an impact outside of the typically loyal German, Austrian and Scandinavian markets.

It was a surprise top ten hit in South Africa, the first hit for Sweet there since 'Fox On The Run' two years previously. According to Connolly, however, by this time, the band were not particularly expecting the singles they released to be hits, nor were they anticipating RCA putting much effort into promoting them. The band's record contract with RCA was soon coming to an end and it was made clear to Sweet that it was not going to be renewed. In subsequent interviews, Connolly maintained that the main motivation for producing this, and their final RCA single, was to signal the band's potential for the benefit of other labels. Although 'Fever of Love' and the following one 'Stairway To The Stars' would sink like stones in terms of chart action, there may have been method in the madness because the band would sign a deal with Polydor that year and their first-ever single for the new label the following year would be a massive hit.

The-B side of 'Fever Of Love' is a heavy but plodding instrumental track: 'A Distinct Lack of Ancient'. The title originates via an in-joke the band had for the name of their favourite pharmaceutical stimulant at the time: 'Old Charles' or 'Ancient Charles'. The track was thus christened on a day when supplies of 'the ancient' in the studio had run completely dry. From a band that had prided themselves on their innovative, carefully-honed, killer B-sides, this track is the archetypal B-side as filler.

Album Release
Off The Record

Personnel:

Brian Connolly: lead vocals

Steve Priest: bass guitar, harmonica, lead and backing vocals

Andy Scott: guitar, keyboards, synthesisers, backing vocals

Mick Tucker: drums, percussion, backing vocals

Produced at Audio International Studios and Kingsway Recorders, London, October 1976-January 1977 by Sweet

UK release date: April 1977

Highest chart places: UK: Did not chart, Germany: 11, US: 151

Running time: 38:32

Recorded mainly in the latter part of 1976, Sweet's fifth studio album was finally released in April 1977. In his autobiography, Priest explains that much of the writing had to be done in the studio as there was little in the way of songs already prepared. He also points out that cocaine was an ever-constant presence by then. Musically, the album can be seen as a natural progression from *Give Us A Wink* rather than a wholesale change in direction. *Off The Record* comes with a glossier production sheen than its predecessor, with fewer hard edges and a good deal more bombast. You can almost sense the cocaine oozing from its tracks.

That theme is very much carried through to the sleeve, a gatefold affair opening out to reveal a stylised close-up of a huge stylus gliding along the grooves of a long-playing record like a spaceship coming into land. While there are not exactly lines of white powder flowing out of each groove, the stylus is clearly seen to be mounted on a golden cocaine spoon. 'Live For Today' was the original working title, after one of the tracks, but *Off The Record* emerged as the chosen title once the idea for the artwork materialised. The initial concept came from a sketch by studio tape operator Norman Goodman, who also gets a design credit on the sleeve alongside the artist himself, Terry Pastor. It is a beautifully executed piece of artwork and makes for a stylish cover, whatever one's opinion of rock star excesses involving Class A drugs. The inside sleeve art carries an action shot of each band member on stage in a perfectly period blend of orange and brown, the de rigueur interior design choice of just about every home in the land in the mid-1970s.

'Fever Of Love' (Connolly / Priest / Scott / Tucker)
'Fever Of Love' had been the most recent single (reviewed earlier in this chapter) and released a couple of months before the album with only limited success. Here, however, it makes for a strong album opener.

'Lost Angels' (Connolly / Priest / Scott / Tucker)
The album then moves on to the other recently-released single 'Lost Angels' which had been put out in October (reviewed in the previous chapter). Had the band tried this trick a couple of years previously, there would have been a danger of the album sounding more like a greatest hits collection, but there was no risk of that now. The tracks are not so well known as standalone singles that they skew the overall flow of the album and this song works far better as an album track anyway.

'Midnight To Daylight' (Connolly / Priest / Scott / Tucker)
The first track on the album that had not been released as a single, it is another of those Sweet songs where Tucker's drumming remains so thunderous throughout it is almost like a continuous drum solo. Although the harmony vocals are less prominent on this track, apart from on the obvious chorus lines, one instrument that does make a rare but very welcome appearance is the harmonica, played by Steve Priest – just as he did on those early session singles he did before joining Sweet. Lyrically, it is more raunchy, standard rock and roll smut, typical for many Sweet songs of this period.

'Windy City' (Connolly / Priest / Scott / Tucker)
Eschewing the more obvious commercial hooks while still going for
a killer riff, 'Windy City' is polished, hard-rocking, album-orientated
Sweet at its best. Inspired by the band's experiences in Chicago on the
1976 tour, it is the longest track on the album, coming in at over seven
minutes. Mid-way through, it veers into an instrumental break where
Tucker and Scott battle it out for supremacy before going into a slightly
sinister-sounding mellow section, prior to all four coming back to
deliver the remainder of the song with righteous fury. The riff has often
drawn comparisons with Deep Purple's 'Woman From Tokyo', but once
the opening verse kicks in, the band carve out their own unequivocal
direction with such powerful delivery that any similarities are soon
forgotten. The song has always remained relatively little-known with
the wider public, but it is no surprise that, over time, the track became
firmly established as a fan favourite. Indeed, outside of the big hits, it
remains one of the songs that Andy Scott's continuing version of Sweet
is frequently pressed by fans to retain in the set-list. It still makes the
occasional appearance.

'Live For Today' (Connolly / Priest / Scott / Tucker)
Starting off as one of those dramatically bombastic introductions that
Sweet had perfected so well over the years, 'Live For Today' is a gloriously
rebellious rock and roll anthem, like a kind of post-adolescent 'Teenage
Rampage' for those self-same kids as they now enter their late teens and
early adulthood. 'Live for today – don't need your politician. Live for
today – don't want no inquisition. Live for today – you gotta throw the
rules away.' Connolly vents with undisguised fury as the band power him
along. A glorious track and one of the album's real highlights. It was going
to be the title track prior to the final cover art concept materialising.

'She Gimme Lovin'' (Connolly / Priest / Scott / Tucker)
Beginning with another explosive drum intro from Tucker, 'She Gimme
Lovin'' is a hard rocker delivered at breakneck speed. The pace slows
down mid-way through for a Zeppelin-esque vocal and rhythm-style jam
before speeding up, once again, for the climax of the song. More cock-
rock lyrics with Connolly in full throttle.

'Laura Lee' (Connolly / Priest / Scott / Tucker)
If there is one minor complaint about the previous *Give Us A Wink*

album, it is that there is little in the way of light and shade. On this later album, 'Laura Lee' provides a welcome change of pace. Beginning as a gentle acoustic ballad with just Connolly's voice and Scott's acoustic guitar, Tucker then comes in to signal the build-up to the majestic chorus of what is a beautiful love song. The track is not a million miles away from the type of material the band would explore more fully on the following album, *Level Headed*. However, to remind us that this is a hard rock album and to tell us that the band are about to take us back into that world, the love song segues into a harder-edged instrumental passage where Scott picks up his electric guitar, once again, and delivers a Stonesy-type riff reminiscent of 'Jumping Jack Flash'. Indeed, when it was originally recorded, the track comprised two separate songs, 'Laura Lee' and 'Show Me The Way', but was cut short for the final release, leaving just the first song and the instrumental break. 'Show Me The Way', replete with the Stonesy-type riff, eventually resurfaced as the B-side to 'California Nights' the following year.

'Hard Times' (Connolly / Priest / Scott / Tucker)

After 'Funk It Up', this is my least favourite track on the album. The ingredients are all there for a great Sweet hard rock song: killer riffs, powerhouse drums, great vocals that combine power-hungry aggression and sweet-sounding harmonies. However, the song lacks the irresistible hooks that make up much of the rest of the album and which are such an integral part of what Sweet is all about. As such, it remains a great track rather than an outstanding one. Lyrically, 'Hard Times' picks up on similar themes explored in 'Action' – overly-demanding record companies, band frustrations with management and the constant pressure to come up with a hit. Priest: 'Every idea or at least nearly every idea we came out with was not good enough in their tin ears.'

'Funk It Up' (Connolly / Priest / Scott / Tucker)

A highly acquired taste for a Sweet number, I made my feelings more than clear in the single review for the previous chapter when this first appeared as a B-side. The only thing I can add by way of mitigation is to praise the immense foresight of the band in placing this last in the running order, so at least it makes it far easier to skip.

The US version of the album released by Capitol had a slightly different track ordering and a remixed version of 'Fever Of Love' with a different intro, as well as the inclusion of an additional song, 'Stairway To The Stars'. This would not appear on the RCA version, where instead, it would be released as a stand-alone, non-album single later in the year. The cover art for the Capitol album was identical, save for the album title appearing on the front of the Capitol version, not just the band's name.

When *Give Us A Wink* was released, even though it had flopped in Britain, the band could at least content themselves with the fact that the album was a hit in the US, where the band were becoming a significant presence. With *Off The Record,* there was no such consolation. As they were pretty much expecting, the album bombed in the UK. However, even though it sold sizeable quantities in the still-loyal German and Scandinavian markets when it came to the US this time, it barely even registered, scraping in at just 151 in the Billboard charts and then disappearing. The band did, at least, garner some decent reviews here and there. Geoff Barton at *Sounds* praised the band's hard-rocking sounds and perfect reproduction that he believed should finally establish Sweet 'as a force to be reckoned with.' US reviewer, Toby Goldstein, was less impressed, however, writing in *Crawdaddy!:* 'The Sweet, in their haste to stand as a non-bubblegum band, have moved away from pop too fast and too far. Their wall-thick harmonies are now at extremes, either as shrill as Freddie Mercury or as non-melodic as Slade. The thing is, both of those acts have already copyrighted their respective styles — there's no need for Sweet to retread tired ground.'

If the band's ambitions had been firmly focused on the US market, where they were less tarred by the glam brush and could enjoy more mainstream rock credibility, it all looked like it was starting to unravel somewhat by 1977. Although Sweet had vowed the previous year to stick to headline tours in the US, even if it meant smaller venues, they had subsequently relented and agreed to a tour that May in support of Aerosmith. Although it was a support slot, Aerosmith in the States were absolutely huge and it would mean the band was playing stadiums and arenas, gaining access to audiences in the tens of thousands. Only weeks before the tour was due to start, however, the band pulled out and Nazareth were hastily called upon to fill the slot vacated by Sweet. 'We were whacked, tired and we were sick of us,' Scott later explained, alluding to rising tensions in the Sweet camp.

Such an apparently suicidal career decision would end up having unexpectedly fortuitous consequences for the band's commercial and creative renaissance the following year, however. Only weeks after the cancelled tour was due to take place, and less than two months after the release of *Off The Record*, the band decamped to Clearwell Castle in the Gloucestershire countryside to begin writing their next album. The change in record labels meant that not only had they been expected to deliver a final studio album for RCA, but they were now also expected to deliver an album for their new label, Polydor too. Priest: 'After the failure of *Off The Record*, it was decided that we should take a different tack with the next album. Someone had heard that Deep Purple had written their last album at a manor house called Clearwell Castle. If it was good enough for them, it must be good enough for us.'

Of course, bands 'getting it together in the country' was not confined to Sweet and Purple and had been going on for a decade or so, with the likes of Traffic, Led Zeppelin and Fairport Convention booking themselves a remote place to experiment with new sounds and explore other musical directions. Tucker in *Blockbuster: The True Story of The Sweet*: 'The whole idea was to get away from hard rock. That had turned into a completely fucking one-way street for us.'

The band had a four-week stay at Clearwell Castle, an eighteenth-century manor house built in medieval style with turrets and mock battlements – nowadays a highly desirable wedding venue. Here, they began working up ideas for the forthcoming album demanded by Polydor. This was then followed by a stay in France to commence recording, once more following in the footsteps of their old friends, Deep Purple. Priest: 'Again, Deep Purple had found a studio at a place called Hérouville, just a few miles outside Paris. It was very picturesque, with a swimming pool and a tennis court.'

Although there were some frustrations with the studio equipment, the consumption of large amounts of alcohol and simmering tensions between Connolly, struggling with some of the vocals, and the rest of the band, the sessions proved extremely productive. The French stay yielded a good chunk of the album before Sweet decamped to the familiar confines of Kingsway Recorders in London.

Single Release
'Stairway To The Stars' (Connolly / Priest / Scott / Tucker)
b/w 'Why Don't You Do It To Me' (Connolly / Priest / Scott / Tucker)
Personnel:

Brian Connolly: lead vocals
Steve Priest: bass guitar, backing vocals
Andy Scott: guitar, keyboards, synthesisers, backing vocals
Mick Tucker: drums, backing vocals
Produced at Kingsway Recorders, London, February 1977 by Sweet
UK release date: August 1977
Highest chart places: UK: Did not chart, Germany: 15, US: Did not chart

The band's final RCA single 'Stairway To The Stars' was recorded back in February 1977 but held back off the UK version of the recent album (even though it appeared on the Capitol version). Opening with a raw-sounding guitar riff rather than the perfectly polished, keyboard-laden intros we had come to expect by this time, listeners could be forgiven for initially thinking this was going to be a more stripped-down offering from Sweet. The track soon transforms into another typically lush production with layer upon layer of vocals, a dreamy acoustic guitar segment and a catchy chorus full of hooks. It could be dismissed as more cocaine-fuelled bombast, but it actually works extremely well, even if it sold extremely poorly. RCA appeared to treat the single as little more than a contractual obligation before the band headed off to Polydor and there was little in the way of promotion. It was a flop almost everywhere, although, once again, the ever-loyal Germans sent the single into the top 20; a lone mark of success for 'Stairway To The Stars'.

The B-side is another non-album track from the sessions earlier in the year: 'Why Don't You Do It To Me'. A strong, pounding rock track with lead vocals shared between Connolly and Priest, it would not have been at all out of place on the recent *Off The Record* album. Given how much importance the band placed on their B-sides in the early stages of their career, it seems quite fitting that their final one for RCA should be more than mere filler, even if very few were destined to hear it at the time.

Once the final RCA single had come and gone, Polydor set about announcing their new signing. The move to Polydor was a little-kept secret anyway and rumours had been circulating in the music press since the start of the year. Polydor issued a press release in September confirming that Sweet were now signed to them for a four-album deal, also confirming that a new album exploring 'new directions' was currently being recorded. With an eye firmly on the band's past, however, RCA released their own compilation that autumn.

Album Release
The Golden Greats

Personnel:

Brian Connolly: lead vocals

Steve Priest: bass guitar, backing vocals

Andy Scott: guitars, keyboards, synthesiser, backing vocals

Mick Tucker: drums, backing vocals

Produced by Phil Wainman (tracks 1-4); Nicky Chinn, Mike Chapman and Phil Wainman (track 5); Nicky Chinn and Mike Chapman (track 6) and Sweet (tracks 7-12).

UK release date: October 1977

Highest chart places: UK: Did not chart, Germany: Did not chart: US: Not released

Running time: 43:22

Tracks listing:

1. Blockbuster! (Chapman / Chinn) 2. Hell Raiser (Chapman / Chinn) 3. Ballroom Blitz (Chapman / Chinn) 4. Teenage Rampage (Chapman / Chinn) 5. The Six Teens (Chapman / Chinn) 6. Turn It Down (Chapman / Chinn) 7. Fox On The Run (Connolly / Priest / Scott / Tucker) 8. Action (Connolly / Priest / Scott / Tucker) 9. Lost Angels (Connolly / Priest / Scott / Tucker) 10. The Lies In Your Eyes (Connolly / Priest / Scott / Tucker) 11. Fever Of Love (Connolly / Priest / Scott / Tucker) 12. Stairway To The Stars (Connolly / Priest / Scott / Tucker)

Sweet's final album while under contract to RCA, was a compilation that brought together the Chinn-Chapman post-bubblegum singles on one side (starting with 'Blockbuster!') and the band's self-written singles on the other (starting with 'Fox On The Run'). For fans who had also purchased The Sweet's *Biggest Hits* five years previously, it would mean that they would now have two companion albums documenting Sweet's entire RCA singles output. While the cover displays a collage of photos of the band members very much in post-glam casual wear, they are set in garish graphics reminiscent of an early 1970s teen pop magazine, spelling out the name of the band. Reviewing the album, *Sounds'* Paul Silverton heaped praise on the Chinn-Chapman side but, apart from 'Fox On The Run' was downbeat about the remainder: 'Really Sweet died in 1974, but in two short years they put out more classic pop singles than Bolan managed in twice as long.' The album did not chart.

After filming promotional videos for the forthcoming releases that would be coming out in the New Year, Sweet spent the latter part of 1977 at Shepperton Studios in Surrey rehearsing for the tour to promote the forthcoming Polydor album. The band had not played live on stage since the Japanese tour back in August 1976. There was new material to work up into a live show and two new guest musicians, Gary Moberly and Nico Ramsden, to induct into the set-up. It is possible to hear the results of these sessions, as an album was eventually released by Angel Air in 2014 from tapes supplied by Scott. The emphasis is firmly on the post-Chinn-Chapman, band-written material. The presence of Ramsden and, in particular, Moberly certainly brings additional texture to the band's live sound, even though Moberly opts for a curiously understated keyboard intro to 'Fox On The Run'. However, although the mellower, prog-influenced material from the forthcoming album features heavily and marks a significant change in direction, there is no dramatic makeover of the earlier hard rock material. Tracks like 'Action' and 'Windy City' are still delivered as crunching, raucous hard rock / heavy metal tracks. Connolly clearly struggles a little with the vocals on some of the rockier tracks, though, with the formerly golden voice turning into more of a strained yell in places. At this point, however, he is still clearly in the game as a talented rock singer. How long that would last would soon become apparent.

Chapter Ten: 1978 – Oxygen

With a fresh new album about to be released, a new sound and a new record company eager to promote it, 1978 looked to be a very promising year for Sweet. Things would go drastically wrong later, of course, but the year began better than any of them could possibly have imagined.

Single Release
'Love Is Like Oxygen' (Scott / Griffin) b/w 'Cover Girl'
(Connolly / Priest / Scott / Tucker)
Personnel:
Brian Connolly: lead vocals
Steve Priest: bass guitar, backing vocals
Andy Scott: guitar, backing vocals
Mick Tucker: drums, backing vocals
Additional personnel:
Geoff Westley: keyboards and arrangements
Produced at Kingsway Recorders, London, Summer-Autumn 1977 by Sweet
UK release date: January 1978
Highest chart places: UK: 9, Germany: 10, US: 8

Although 'Love Is Like Oxygen' began taking shape while the band were out in France recording the *Level Headed* album, it was one of the songs that was not recorded until they got back to England later that summer. Scott: 'The seed of the idea came from Trevor Griffin, who was our sound engineer. He was a pretty good pianist. I kept hearing bits when we were in the studio or whenever there was a piano around, he would start fiddling and I'd heard two or three bits of the song or the ideas that might be able to be knitted together. So, having done that, I sat with a cassette and worked out that this could be a verse and that could be an intro.'

In his autobiography, Priest states that after Griffin's initial piano ideas had been pulled together into an arrangement by Westley, the four members were all ordered by Scott to go away and try and come up with some lyrics. Priest: 'I wrote something totally forgettable and the idea was thrown out immediately. Andy had gone home and listened to Hall & Oates, who had 'inspired' him. I'll let the reader figure out which album he had been listening to. As I have mentioned before, plagiarism is part of the music business. Mick and I did think that this was a bit blatant, though, but we couldn't come up with anything better.'

The Hall & Oates song that Priest is hinting at here is 'Grounds for Separation' from their 1975 self-titled studio album. It includes the following lyrics in the bridge:

Music, it's my life and I've got it in me
But isn't it a bit like oxygen, 'cause too much will make you high
But not enough will make you die
So I gotta keep it under control

It does, indeed, bear striking similarities to the chorus of 'Love Is Like Oxygen':

Love is like oxygen
You get too much, you get too high
Not enough and you're gonna die

The two remain quite different songs, though and apart from obvious similarities in the lyrics they do not have much in common with one another at all, besides both being part of the mid to late 1970s soft rock canon. Moreover, while the lyrics of the Hall & Oates song are clearly referring to music, Scott's focus is very much on love and romance. Scott, himself, explains things rather differently to Priest: 'I'd already dug out some lyrics that I'd written two or three years earlier. Basically, all I'd written down was, 'Love is like oxygen, you get too much, you get too high, not enough and you're gonna die. Love gets you high,' and I was determined that these were the lyrics that are going to fit this.'

Expanding on those lyrics and utilising the arrangement skills of Westley, the song came together as the most magnificent mini-symphony. From the majestic keyboard intro to the way the guitar riff interacts with the rhythmic double arpeggio piano to the spellbinding vocals, the band had created a masterpiece. While the troubled Connolly was not required for the song's high choruses, for the verses, he managed to deliver a vocal performance that would remain one of the highlights of his career. Scott said in *Classic Rock* magazine in 2017: 'The verses in Oxygen … the ones that Brian sang were some of the best he'd done in years.'

From the very early stages, Polydor executives were expressing immense enthusiasm about the song as a potential single, but at nearly seven minutes, this symphonic, proggish, pop masterpiece was far too long for a single, so it was edited down to a more radio-friendly 3:48 minutes by losing the extended instrumental passages. Released in early January, by mid-January, Sweet were back on *Top Of The Pops*. By the end of January, the single had broken into the top 40 and by mid-February, it had achieved what many would have predicted would now be impossible, getting Sweet back into the UK top ten. It was received with similar enthusiasm across the world, reaching the top ten in the US, Australia and swathes of mainland Europe. Later in the year, the song would secure an Ivor Novello nomination as well as an Ascap Award in the US. Quite possibly the most fantastic piece of music someone has ever written for a band that they roadie for in the history of popular music.

'Cover Girl', with its pounding riff like a speeded-up 'Spirit In The Sky' on acid, shows that the band could still come up with some great surprises on their B-sides. Much rockier than anything on the actual album, it is as if the band vent all their excess hard rock energy on a powerful, hard-riffing B-side – just as they did in the early bubblegum days with Chinn-Chapman.

Album Release
Level Headed

Personnel:

Brian Connolly: lead vocals (except tracks 1, 3 and 5), backing vocals

Steve Priest: bass guitar, synthesiser voice, lead vocals (track 3), backing vocals

Andy Scott: guitar, synthesiser, lead vocals (tracks 1 and 5), backing vocals

Mick Tucker: drums, percussion, backing vocals

Additional personnel:

Ronnie Asprey: brass

Richard Harvey: baroque wind

Stevie Lange: vocals (track 8)

Geoff Westley: keyboards, string arrangements

Produced at Château d'Hérouville, France and Kingsway Recorders, London, Summer-Autumn 1977 by Sweet

UK release date: January 1978

Highest chart places: UK: Did not chart, Germany: 15, US: 52

Running time: 39:53

Released the same month as the single and launched at a press conference on 19 January at London's Mayfair Hotel, *Level Headed* is almost as much of a musical departure from its predecessor *Off The Record* as *Sweet Fanny Adams* was from its predecessor *Funny How Sweet Co-Co Can Be* back in the early 1970s.

Although Priest and sometimes Scott had, on occasion, taken lead vocals on previous albums (particularly on *Sweet Fanny Adams* as a result of Connolly's throat injury), such were band politics and the creative modus operandi when *Level Headed* was being produced that Connolly was no longer regarded as the automatic choice for lead vocals when songs were being assembled. Accordingly, of the ten tracks on the album, just five of them are credited to Connolly as lead vocalist. Scott gets two, Priest gets two, albeit one of those is a synthesiser voice run through a repeat tape loop, and the remaining track is an instrumental. Unlike previous albums, certainly since the very early days, there is also a significant cast of supporting musicians. Musician and composer Geoff Westley (who has worked with everyone from the Bee Gees to Andrew Lloyd Weber to Henry Mancini) was brought in to provide keyboards and string arrangements. Jazz rock alto-sax player, Ronnie Asprey, plays brass and Richard Harvey who had been in prog rock outfit Gryphon and whose mastery of baroque wind instruments was key to that band's highly distinctive medieval/renaissance sound, also came in to work similar magic for Sweet.

While the album was recorded in France and London, that place in Gloucestershire where the band did much of their writing and which helped establish the general template for the album, Clearwell Castle, also gets a special credit on the sleeve: 'for an expensive but inspiring twenty-eight days.'

The cover art for the RCA release is a grainy monochrome picture of the four members, including a now-bearded Scott, adopting a suitably AOR pose with pale T-shirts and serious expressions. The portrait was taken by photographer Dick Barnatt, who visited the band at Kingsway Recorders as they were putting the final touches to album. The photo session was arranged during a break for lunch, with Connolly seen still holding his mug of tea on the album cover. The Capitol artwork, meanwhile, follows on from the theme of the previous year's *Off The Record* with a play on the words in the title and a close-up drawing of a set of tape heads as part of some futuristic landscape. On the RCA version, the tape head artwork would be relegated to the inner part of the gatefold sleeve, with the inside cover sleeve finally revealing that the cassette tape heads are actually part of a stylised electric guitar. The Capitol release also carried a quite different running order and some totally unnecessary pruning of one track, 'Fountain'.

'Dream On' (Scott)

From the delicate opening piano refrain to hearing the voice of Scott rather than Connolly to lyrics that form the basis of a deeply tender love song rather than rock 'n' roll shenanigans involving groupies and gang-bangs, the listener is instantly alerted to the fact that the album they are about to hear will be quite unlike any Sweet album that has gone before it. Written by Scott alone, 'Dream On' is said to be inspired by a girl that he had fallen for while at Clearwell and who subsequently came out and spent time with him at Hérouville. One of the softest and gentlest songs on the entire album, it sends out a very strong message that Sweet have embarked upon a major change in direction.

'Love Is Like Oxygen' (Scott / Griffin)

The version of Sweet's sonic masterpiece that is 'Love Is Like Oxygen' is considerably longer here than what was released as the single. There is an extended instrumental break mid-way through where Scott gets to explore his classical guitar fantasies. Scott: 'We were working with an arranger, Geoff Westley, who was a fantastic pianist with his Rachmaninov-style piano and for me to put some Julian Bream and John Williams-style classical, gut-strung guitar with his piano work was just fantastic.' The classically influenced acoustic passage then segues into an extended electric rock section before returning back to the main chorus. Finally, during the last minute of the song funk and disco influences come to the fore with another instrumental section. The entire extended track again reinforces to listeners that Sweet are on a very different journey with this album.

'California Nights' (Connolly / Priest / Scott / Tucker)

A sentiment clearly close to his heart given that he would soon be leaving Britain for good and settling in the States with his new partner, Maureen, it is no surprise that Priest opted to provide the lead vocal on this track, rather than Connolly. 'I never thought I would end up living in California, but I always wanted to,' Priest reflected in his autobiography, looking back to the time spent recording this song. A slightly shorter, edited version of the track would later be released as the second single from the album, as a follow-up to 'Love Is Like Oxygen'. It is quite a different beast, however. For all the prog-inclined pomp of 'Love Is Like Oxygen,' this is Sweet doing the sort of sun-drenched, West Coast, easy-going, countrified pop-rock that the likes of the Eagles had perfected. In his solo ahead of the final choruses, Scott even gets to add a spot of Americana-sounding guitar.

'Strong Love' (Connolly / Priest / Scott / Tucker)

Following the previous year's 'Funk It Up' on *Off The Record*, 'Strong Love' is another funk-based track dominated by a throbbing disco beat. Priest caustically remarks in his autobiography that the initial idea was Scott's after listening to a lot of Hall & Oates and deciding that 'he was England's version of Blue Eyed Soul'. Like its 'Funk It Up' predecessor, this one is skilfully executed and, in a further example of Sweet's desire to spread their wings musically, jazz rock alto-sax player, Ronnie Asprey, is brought in to add further texture with some cool-sounding brass. Sadly, however, like 'Funk It Up', the whole thing leaves me utterly cold.

'Fountain' (Connolly / Priest / Scott / Tucker)

Another gentle love song in the soft-rock vein, 'Fountain' is the second one where Scott gets the lead vocal credit. Two things make this track really stand out so that it becomes far more than just an acoustic guitar track with a pleasant melody. The first is a blinding electric guitar solo and the second is the harpsichord. While both the lyrics and the guitar solo were Scott's, it was Priest's idea to have that distinctive harpsichord interlude in the final minute of the track. They were certainly getting their money's worth out of arranger Westley on this album.

'Anthem No. I (Lady Of The Lake)' (Connolly / Priest / Scott / Tucker)

This was another of the early songs to emerge out of the Clearwell Castle writing sessions. 'This song was very much influenced by our surroundings,' wrote Priest. Connolly elaborated further, telling journalists at the album's press launch that the castle reminded him of King Arthur and the legend of the sword in the lake. Lyrically, it was certainly a contrast from the tales of groupies, sex and street fights that had dominated previous albums. Some of the band's past material did provide a glimmer of what was to come, however, particularly some of Scott's earlier writing. 'Lady Starlight' and 'Medusa' were not a million miles away from what we were now seeing on *Level Headed*, both lyrically and in terms of overall feel, even if they lacked the elaborate string arrangements and orchestration. There have been a few sly digs at the lyrics over the years. 'You are the queen, I'm just a pawn, in the chess game of life,' is hardly Chaucer, but they captured a mood – and that was really what mattered at the time.

'Silverbird' (Connolly / Priest / Scott / Tucker)

After the renaissance-flavoured, proggy, art-rock indulgence of the previous track, the band return with some more straight-ahead, radio-friendly pop-rock. Connolly is sounding in fine voice. It is clear that this type of mid-paced material is suiting him, with no obvious sign that he is struggling with any of the vocals here. Just to remind us that Sweet have not gone too soft, though, Tucker's drums become much more prominent – another one of those nice memorable little touches on this album.

'Lettres D'Amour' (Connolly / Priest / Scott / Tucker)

Just as the turreted, fairy-tale castle surroundings of Clearwell inspired songs like 'Lady of the Lake', the subsequent relocation to France inspired 'Lettres D'Amour' – conceived after a trip out to Paris, according to Priest. Written as a duet, the renowned session singer, Stevie Lange (former wife of legendary producer Mutt), provides guest vocals on this track. Sharing lead vocals with Connolly, she is the first female vocalist to grace a Sweet recording since the days of The Lady Birds backing singers on Sweet's final Parlophone single back in 1970.

'Anthem No. II' (Connolly / Priest / Scott / Tucker)

Priest wrote in *Are You Ready Steve?* that the band liked the string arrangement from 'Anthem No. I' so much that they were moved to record it again as an instrumental. Wonderfully bonkers and unlike anything ever heard on a Sweet album before, hearing that beautiful melody and Westley's enchanting string arrangement reprised for a short one-minute musical interlude simply adds to *Level Headed's* overall eccentric charm. The fact that the band were still short of material and had yet to come up with the album's centre-piece and lead single, 'Love Is Like Oxygen' at the time they recorded this probably also played a part in their decision to include it.

'Air On 'A' Tape Loop' (Priest / Scott / Tucker)

Rather than being recorded at Hérouville, this was one of the tracks that were put together at Kingsway Recorders after the band returned to London. The title is fairly self-explanatory. It is a track created from a tape loop with the main vocal simply being Priest repeating the words 'alpha beta gamma delta' over and over while other-worldly guitars, sinister-sounding synthesisers and swirling special effects play over a hypnotic rhythm from Priest and Tucker. Priest: 'Mick and I put down about twenty seconds of the backtrack and Louis Austin made it into a loop. He then copied it onto another two-inch tape. We had no idea of what tune to play over it. One evening while listening to 'Solveg's Song' from the Peer Gynt Suite, I knew that tune would fit. With a little imagination, it did.' Over the years, the track has drawn comparisons with everything from Kraftwerk to the Alan Parsons Project, to *Meddle*-era Pink Floyd, while studio engineer, Austin, said the tape loop process itself was inspired by 10cc's 'I'm Not In Love'. For an album that so often delves deep into past musical traditions and ancient myths, 'Air On 'A' Tape Loop' ensures *Level Head*ed ends on a surprisingly futuristic note – at least for 1978.

With the single 'Love Is Like Oxygen' being so fantastically well received, promotion for the album could not have got off to a better start. Reviews were generally very favourable. *Record Mirror's* John Shearlaw praised the band for being 'cool, calm and collected' in producing what he called 'a clever rock album' – predicting that the album would be enormously successful. *Sounds*, too, were enthusiastic. *NME*, of course, while responding favourably to the lead single, were characteristically scathing when it came to the album as a whole. In the US, both *Billboard* and *Rolling Stone* magazine were also enthusiastic, the latter pouring cold water on the band's post-glam, hard rock stylings and much preferring this new softer direction.

Sales, however, were mixed. While the album made the top 40 in Australia and several European countries, it only made no. 52 in the US Billboard charts, a vast improvement on sales of *Off The Record* but still failing to match the stateside success of *Give Us A Wink*. Yet again, the album failed to chart at all in the UK. Being such a departure from what had been released previously, the album, 'Love Is Like Oxygen' aside, also appeared to greatly divide the remaining Sweet fans. Retrospectively, however, it has gone on to garner critical appreciation in many unlikely quarters. Even the UK's *Prog Magazine* ran a fulsome tribute to *Level Headed* back in 2019.

In support of the album, a European tour had been put together, taking in Spain, Switzerland, Austria, Germany, Denmark and Sweden throughout late January and early to mid-February. Nine days later, this was followed by a single, one-off UK date at London's Hammersmith Odeon on 24 February. This would be the first live gig that Sweet had played on British soil since they played the Isle of Man back in July 1975 and the first Sweet gig on the British mainland since they ended their winter UK tour in Southend on 13 December 1974. It was quite some gap. The show was a sell-out.

Priest: 'When we took to the stage, the suspense was incredible. We opened with what had become our anthem, 'Ballroom Blitz'. The crowd went nuts. I have never seen a crowd in London react this way.' Connolly: 'It was the best thing that has ever happened in my life.' The reviews in the ever-fickle British music press were fulsome with their praise, with *Melody Maker* declaring that everything went right for them and 'you could take the band seriously'. As Priest noted in his autobiography, Hammersmith would be the last time England ever saw the Sweet in its original form.

The successful European tour and the Hammersmith triumph were then followed by a US tour beginning in late March. It was not just Britain and mainland Europe that had been waiting a good while for Sweet to get on stage again. It had been two years since they had last played the US, too. The US dates were in two legs. The first chunk was in late March, all of April and early May and would then be followed by a second chunk covering late May, June and early July. The first leg was a significant, high-volume tour in terms of ticket sales, where they were touring in support of the stadium-filling Bob Seger. Most of it passed by without incident and it helpfully exposed Sweet to US audiences in the tens of thousands. A disastrous date in Birmingham, Alabama, on 3 May 1978 became legendary; however, in a career that had never been entirely free of disasters. Connolly's drinking had got so completely out of hand that he was simply incapable of performing that night. Moreover, this was on a night when big-wigs from the band's US label, Capitol Records, had flown over specially to see the band perform at what was supposed to be a hugely prestigious gig.

Tucker, interviewed in October 1989, a decade after Connolly's departure from the band but some years prior to his death: 'I think it's safe to say this now, but Brian had a drink problem that he didn't realise he had and it's a sickness. Alcoholism is a sickness. And I think it culminated in one very bad experience on one of the dates we did. It was Birmingham, Alabama and I think Brian was taking some medication. I don't know. But we did a show. We were on the Bob Seger tour and he didn't know where he was. And there were a lot of record company people there and all hell broke loose after that.' Scott: 'Our manager pulled him off the stage and we finished the set as a three-piece.' Priest: 'The next day, when some of the dust had settled, we had a meeting that would start crumbling the foundations of the band. Andy wanted to throw Brian out of the band then and there.'

Things were patched up sufficiently to continue the final dates of the first leg of the tour, even though, once again, there was an issue with Connolly's drunkenness at the final gig on 6 May in Atlanta. The band then flew back to England and an urgent band meeting with manager, David Walker, which resulted in a commitment to commence work on a second album for Polydor just as soon as the dates on the second leg of the US tour had been fulfilled.

In his autobiography, Priest is emphatic that the band's fortunes could have been much altered had they continued to undertake more US dates in support of the *Level Headed* album and thus repair their relations with Capitol. How the band could have carried on successfully touring when things were so volatile and Connolly's problems with alcohol addiction so evident, however, is anybody's guess.

Single Release
'California Nights' (Connolly / Priest / Scott / Tucker) b/w
'Show Me The Way' (Connolly / Priest / Scott / Tucker)
Personnel:
Brian Connolly: lead vocals (B-side only), backing vocals
Steve Priest: bass guitar, lead vocals, backing vocals
Andy Scott: guitar, synthesiser, backing vocals
Mick Tucker: drums, backing vocals
Produced at: Produced at Château d'Hérouville, France and Kingsway Recorders, London, Summer-Autumn 1977 by Sweet b/w Produced at Audio International Studios and Kingsway Recorders, London, 1976 by Sweet
UK release date: May 1978
Highest chart places: UK: Did not chart, Germany: 23, US: 76

Connolly was still in the band when the next single was released but tellingly, and perhaps prophetically, it was Priest, not Connolly, who was singing lead vocal. 'California Nights' makes for a good song on the *Level Headed* album. As a single, though, without Connolly's vocal (even if only for part of the record like on 'Love Is Like Oxygen'), Sweet lose a big part of what makes them Sweet. As a lead vocalist Priest's voice is pleasantly agreeable rather than stunningly distinctive.

Chart-wise, it was as if 'Love Is Like Oxygen' had never happened: a lowly no. 76 in the US and an even more miserable no. 86 in Canada.

Even the usually-loyal German market could not quite push the single into the top 20, and it rested just outside at no. 23.

The B-side 'Show Me The Way' would be the final release to carry a Connolly lead vocal while he was still a member of the band. A harder-edged rock song with a Stonesy-type riff and an angry vocal from Connolly, one can see it would be out of place on the *Level Headed* album and was the type of material more readily suited to the previous couple of albums. Indeed, the song was originally destined to appear on the *Off The Record* album as part of an extended medley with the track 'Laura Lee' but was eventually edited down and did not make the final cut.

The band resumed the second part of their US tour in late May, where they had support slots with such hard rock titans as Rush, Cheap Trick, REO Speedwagon and Alice Cooper. Once the US tour was concluded, the band then returned to the UK and began preparing for another album. Gary Moberly remained involved providing keyboards but not Nico Ramsden, who was surplus to requirements once the US tour concluded. Once again, the band booked a month-long stay at Clearwell Castle. There would be no expressions of gratitude on the album sleeve notes this time, however. Priest called it 'a disastrous time'. Although some songs did get written and some demos were laid down during this period, Connolly's drinking was sadly out of control. As well as continuing tensions between Connolly and Scott, there were also reports of Connolly's general estrangement from the rest of the band.

Following the stay at Clearwell through late August and most of September, the band booked Townhouse Studios in London's Shepherd's Bush to begin recording the album that would become *Cut Above The Rest*, commencing in late October. Here, the problems with Connolly became even more evident. Connolly managed to lay down the vocals for just two songs at Townhouse: 'Play All Night' and 'That Girl'. The latter would eventually morph into the track 'Stay With Me' when the Connolly-less Sweet released the final version on their new album the following year.

The two tracks sung by Connolly were eventually released almost two decades later as part of the *Platinum Rare* collection in 1995. When I bought this at the time, my first reaction was that Connolly's voice sounded pretty good. Even if they were not up to the standard of 'Blockbuster!' or 'The Six Teens', the recordings are in no way comparable to later recordings of Connolly's in the 1980s, where he struggles his way through a number of old Sweet hits. In his autobiography, however, Priest explains that it took a whole week for Connolly just to lay down the vocals on one track. Obviously, in any commercial studio setting, time is money and it cannot remain a viable situation for very long to have a lead singer who struggles so much to put down a vocal. Less than two weeks after recording for the new album had commenced, Connolly was out of the band. His departure was not announced immediately and for the time being, the remaining members decided to carry on recording the album as a three-piece.

In the years that followed, there were conspiracy theories put about, including by Sweet's former manager David Walker, that the band deliberately sabotaged Connolly's attempts to sing by choosing to record the album in a key that he would not be able to handle. It seems quite an elaborate and dastardly plot for any band to dream up and it is a rumour that Scott is quick to refute. Scott: 'This isn't Supertramp where the guitars aren't important enough ... This is the stuff that works in E, A and B. And certain riffs have to be done in a certain way.'

1978 began with so much promise for Sweet, but as the year ended, greater uncertainty hung over the band's future than at any time previously. With hindsight, maybe the best thing the band could have done is take a break for a couple of years. This could have given them time to find a new lead singer or even for Connolly to be given the type of support he needed to overcome his addictions. Then the band could have bounced back in the early 1980s, refreshed and alert, ready to ride renewed interest stoked up by the New Wave Of British Heavy Metal and the emerging US glam metal scene. That was not the route that was taken, however, and 1979 would throw up its own challenges and frustrations.

Chapter Eleven: 1979 – Then There Were Three

If 1970 was the year when things began to fall into place for The Sweet, 1979 was certainly the year when everything began to unravel. It would turn out to be a desperately challenging year for the band in a whole number of ways.

As the year began, Connolly's exit had not been announced and the three remaining members continued work on the new album at Townhouse studios as a three-piece, together with studio guests, namely keyboard player Gary Moberly and, once again, pianist and arranger, Geoff Westley. The band were also still chewing over their longer-term options regarding a lead vocalist. The idea of a replacement for Connolly was discussed and various singers were mooted including, apparently, Ronnie James Dio, who had left Rainbow but had yet to join Black Sabbath. Regardless of what conversations took place between the Sweet camp and Dio and regardless of how serious a prospect of him joining was, Sweet nevertheless took the decision to continue as a three-piece.

In his autobiography, Priest states that a possible change of name was also mooted, with S. T. P. (Scott Tucker Priest) being under consideration. Neither the idea of a name change nor hiring a new singer came to fruition. The band would carry on as Sweet, sharing the lead vocals as they had been doing in the sessions for the album.

The news about Connolly leaving was finally made public towards the end of February 1979. A statement issued on 23 February by Sweet manager, David Walker, announced Connolly's departure, utilising that old music industry staple of musical differences 'after long discussions about their musical direction'. Press coverage that week indicated that while Connolly would be pursuing his own direction in a new solo career, he would not be replaced as Sweet's lead singer and the band would, instead, continue as a three-piece. *Record Mirror* carried a quote from Walker saying, 'Brian was a teenybop idol, but as you grow up, you change your attitudes and you want to do something different.' Connolly, himself, was quoted that week: 'Well, I would have, in fact, left two years before I did, but I just stuck out to tour – out of loyalty, I suppose.'

Single Release
'Call Me' (Scott) **b/w 'Why Don't You'** (Priest / Scott / Tucker)
Personnel:
Steve Priest: bass guitar, vocals

Andy Scott: guitar, synthesiser, backing vocals
Mick Tucker: drums, backing vocals
Additional personnel: Gary Moberly: piano
Produced at Townhouse Studio London, 1978-1979 by Sweet
UK release date: March 1979
Highest chart places: UK: Did not chart, Germany: 29, US: Not released

Less than a fortnight after Connolly's departure was finally made public, Sweet fans got the chance to hear the new three-piece version for the first time with the release of the single: 'Call Me'. After the tender love songs and medieval fantasies of the *Level Headed* album, we are back to more traditional rock and roll sleaze and debauchery for this first single from the forthcoming *Cut Above The Rest* album. Sung by Priest and written by Scott, the song is basically about a guy laying on his bed in a hotel room and ordering a call girl. If people assume such lyrics would signal a return to the harder rocking pre- *Level Headed* sound of Sweet, however, they are mistaken. This is very much Sweet in late 1970s synth-heavy, soft rock mode. Indeed, in his autobiography, Priest recalls Tucker dismissing the song as 'pop pap'. The single release is an edited version of the song that appears on the album as the band's management feared the full lyrics would incur the wrath of censors and get it banned from airplay. The most risqué verse is therefore removed from the seven-inch.

Despite the attempt to produce a radio-friendly edit, however, it was a flop pretty much everywhere. Germany bucked the trend and sent it to the lower reaches of the top 30 at no. 29, but even the patience of the ever-loyal Germans was about to snap. This would be the band's final hit single there. Some of the reviews were equally brutal. *Record Mirror*, who had lavished praise on 'Love Is Like Oxygen' and *Level Headed* the year before, responded to the invitation in the title with a simple sarcastic put-down: 'Sure... don't call us!'

Slightly rockier than most of the *Cut Above The Rest* album, the non-album B-side 'Why Don't You' contains some nice lead guitar from Scott. It is worth pointing out that it is a quite different song to 'Why Don't You Do It To Me', which was the B-side to 'Stairway To The Stars' two years previously. It was maybe a sign that in recycling song titles, Sweet were starting to run out of steam, given they would repeat a similar trick the following year when some of the lyrics and half the title of 'Own Up, Take A Look At Yourself' (the B- side to 'Teenage Rampage') would turn up in the guise of a completely different song on the *Water's Edge* album in 1980.

The US Capitol release of *Cut Above The Rest* was released in April 1979 and by June had crawled up to no. 151 in the Billboard album charts – but would go no higher. At least it meant the album was available and in the shops when the band headed out there to promote it with a nineteen-date tour. British and European Sweet fans, meanwhile, would have to wait until October.

Kicking off in New York and eventually winding up in the deep south, the US tour encompassed support slots for Journey and then Cheap Trick, giving the band the opportunity to introduce material from the new album as well as the hits like 'Love Is Like Oxygen' and 'Ballroom Blitz'. Gary Moberly, who had toured with the band the previous year while Connolly was still with them, once again joined for this tour and a second guitarist, Ray McRiner, was also brought in for part of the tour. Another guest musician rather than a permanent member, a couple of McRiner's compositions would appear on the 1980 *Water's Edge* album, even though he was no longer directly involved with the band after the tour.

Following Connolly's departure, the dynamics of the band appeared to be fracturing even further when Priest informed the others that he would be relocating permanently to the US rather than returning to the UK after the tour. Priest was now involved in a serious relationship with Maureen O'Connor, a senior executive with responsibility for publicity and artist relations at Capitol Records. Based in New York, the pair had originally met on Sweet's 1976 US tour and then subsequently reconnected two years later. From this point on, Priest very much saw his future in the US rather than the UK. Following his divorce from his first wife, the two would marry in 1981 and would remain together until Priest's death in 2020.

Single Release
'Big Apple Waltz' (Priest / Scott) b/w 'Why Don't You' (Priest / Scott / Tucker)
Personnel:
Steve Priest: bass guitar, vocals
Andy Scott: guitar, synthesisers, backing vocals
Mick Tucker: drums, backing vocals
Additional personnel:
Geoff Westley: piano, arrangements
Produced at Townhouse Studios London, 1978-1979 by Sweet
UK release date: August 1979
Highest chart places: Did not chart

One of the songs that originally emerged out of the initial album-writing session at Clearwell Castle the previous September, 'Big Apple Waltz' is a song inspired by Priest's blossoming romance with his New York-based partner, Maureen. This lovely piano-based ballad features Priest on vocals and carries more typically melodic lead guitar work from Scott. Regardless of how it works in the context of an album, however, one must really question the judgement of anyone who thought it would cut it as the song to get Sweet back in the charts. Even though the lyrics are a touching declaration of commitment to his new love, Priest was characteristically scathing about the selection of the track for a single, 'It really was a poor choice for a single and I think Walker just picked it to make me happy.'

The single would be a flop everywhere. For the first time since 'Get On The Line' was released back in 1970, an official Sweet release would fail to chart in a single country, with not even those previously loyal Germans buying enough copies to make it a hit.

On the B-side, it was not merely a case of recycling song titles this time; it was actually recycling a song. 'Why Don't You' was the exact same recording of the exact same song that had appeared as the B-side to 'Call Me' earlier in the year. It could be that Polydor had taken the view that so few people had bought 'Call Me' that they would give people a second chance to hear the B-side or it could be that they had simply stopped caring. Scott expressed his frustration with such sloppiness, stating in one interview, 'We've always been a band who will do a B-side. We've never been one to shirk.'

In the latter stages of the 1970s, the band seemed to have stumbled into an operating model where any challenges the band faced – be it declining public appeal, internal tensions or creative differences – the solution always appeared to be the same: go away and record another album. It worked for them with *Level Headed*, following the band's disappointment with how *Off The Record* was received. There was no sign that *Cut Above The Rest* was going to work the same magic or paper over any cracks this time, however. No matter, before the album had even been released in the UK and mainland Europe, Sweet were off to record yet another new album. Following the conclusion of the US tour, the band headed over to Canada, at Eastern Sound Studio in Toronto, to begin recording what would be the *Water's Edge* album. There were obvious tax advantages in recording abroad, which is the key reason *Give Us A Wink* ended up being recorded in Germany and *Level Headed* in France, for example. Initially, it was hoped that the band could make the album in the States, but, no doubt exacerbated by continuing tensions between the band's UK and US management, it became apparent that they had not gone through the necessary bureaucratic hurdles to lessen their tax liabilities. Canada ended up being the next best thing.

This did not mean that things were secure financially, however. The band were landed with a bill for over £500,000 from the Inland Revenue for unpaid taxes. A combination of hugely extravagant lifestyles – even when record sales remained modest, poor management and a top rate of income tax of 83% in 1970s Britain had pretty much done for the band's finances.

Album Release
Cut Above The Rest

Personnel:

Steve Priest: bass, harmonica, lead vocals, backing vocals

Andy Scott: guitar, synthesiser, lead vocals, backing vocals

Mick Tucker: drums, percussion, lead vocals, backing vocals

Additional personnel:

Eddie Hardin: ARP 2600 solo

Gary Moberly: piano

Geoff Westley: piano, arrangements

Produced at Townhouse Studios, London, 1978-1979 by Sweet

UK release date: October 1979 (US release date: March 1979)

Highest chart places: UK: did not chart, Germany: 49, US: 151

Running time: 37:50

The first thing to say about Sweet's final album of the 1970s and the first without Connolly is that it does genuinely suffer from the absence of his voice. Even if Connolly's lead vocal is only on a proportion of the tracks, as on the previous album, and even if, as we also witness on the previous album, he only sings certain parts of particular songs, his voice is still there – an essential part of the overall Sweet sound alongside that beautiful blend of harmonised voices. While his continued membership of Sweet may no longer have been remotely tenable, and while his departure was perhaps utterly inevitable, it does leave quite a significant hole to fill on the album. Scott sings lead on two songs and for the first time ever, Tucker also gets the lead vocal on two tracks. Priest gets the lion's share with five, while he and Scott share lead vocals on another. All three are enjoyable vocalists to listen to, but none of them are Connolly. Certainly, none of them are Connolly in his prime. Where the real magic of Priest's, Scott's and Tucker's voices came from was in their collective ability to add those exquisite Sweet harmonies. Those vocal harmonies backing Connolly was where their voices were perfection rather than merely enjoyable.

The second thing to say about *Cut Above The Rest* is that while *Level Headed* was a major departure from both the glam heyday singles and the hard rock direction of *Give Us A Wink* and *Off The Record*, it could still boast the classic line-up, it could boast a bona fide classic hit single in 'Love Is Like Oxygen' and, importantly, with its baroque musical stylings and symphonic orchestration it still had a flamboyance about it. From bubblegum to glam, to hard rock to baroque prog, flamboyance seemed to be written into the very essence of Sweet's DNA. *Cut Above The Rest*, by contrast, comes across as a very introspective album. Obviously, there is no Brian but there is no particular stand-out single either, certainly nothing on a par with 'Love Is Like Oxygen'. The album does boast some highly enjoyable songs and some interesting musical experimentation in a 10cc / ELO kind of vein. Overall, however, it lacks the energy of its immediate predecessors and too much of it gets caught up in pleasant, but not exactly cutting-edge, soft-rock balladry.

It may not have been the best Sweet album ever recorded, but with sessions at Townhouse studios continuing over several months and with arranger and pianist Geoff Westley, once again on the payroll for this album, Priest wrote that this was probably the most expensive album the band had recorded to date.

The cover art for the Polydor release of *Cut Above The Rest* is a stylised version of a reel-to-reel tape recorder and tape editing block, with a strategically-placed razor blade across a tape that is laden with musical notation. It continues a similar theme as that established with the cover art for *Off The Record* and the Capitol release of *Level Headed*, with a similarly pun-based title to boot. Indeed, the cover illustration is by Norman Goodman, who came up with the original concept for the *Off The Record* sleeve. However, rather than Terry Pastor's beautifully dramatic artistry to bring the final concept to life, Goodman's own slightly more rough and ready technique makes it to the final sleeve here. Moreover, rather than an elegant gatefold sleeve opening out to reveal a panoramic futuristic vision, Polydor's budget seemingly only ran to a standard sleeve with an identical illustration on both sides. A black and white version of the exact same design is again repeated on the inner sleeve along with the credits, with a portrait of the three remaining band members at the studio console on the reverse. Another thing worth noting is the lack of anything approaching a consistent typeface or band logo on any of Sweet's seven studio albums throughout the 1970s. This was not uncommon at the time. Instantly recognisable band logos only really started to become a big thing in the 1980s. Prior to that, bands would often chop and change from album to album. In the US, Capitol opted for a completely different cover for the album, once again, based on a woodcut image of the three band members.

'Call Me' (Scott)

The album opens with the full-length version of 'Call Me', Scott's song about a hooker in a hotel. For the select few who did purchase the original single earlier in the year, they would now be able to find out what the missing verse was, which had been removed from the single lest it offend the censors:

I lay on my belly she rubbed in petroleum jelly
Her hand felt so good
Lie on my back, nearly blowing my stack oh, I wish she would
Surrender the sweets
What she does with her feet
She satisfies and her pocket don't lie
Then she waved her goodbye

The track began life as a song called 'Give Me Your Love'. At Priest's beckoning, however, Scott was persuaded to go away and rewrite it because the lyric was felt to be too similar to the lyrics of 'Cover Girl' (the B-side of 'Love Is Like Oxygen'), which opens with the line 'Give me your love'. You can hear the original demo on the *Platinum Rare* album that was first released in 1995.

'Play All Night' (Priest / Scott / Tucker)

One of the products of the Clearwell Castle writing sessions, 'Play All Night' became one of just two songs that Connolly attempted in the early stages of recording the album prior to his departure. On the Connolly demo, there is a glimmer of the old magic in there, but, sadly, it was not to be. Scott confirms in the *Platinum Rare* sleeve notes that the demo is almost certainly the last thing that Connolly recorded with them. The final released version is sung by Scott and is certainly the heaviest thing on the album. With its chant-like chorus and driving bass-line 'Play All Night' would not have been out of place on one of the band's hard rock albums like *Give Us A Wink*. However, the understated soft-rock production mode means the track never quite reaches its full potential of classic-sounding Sweet in full throttle, even though it is one of the album's stronger tracks. In a parallel universe, I like to think of this song as a sing-along stadium anthem that a refreshed and revived Sweet would blast out to huge audiences across the globe. Maybe with a fully-recovered Connolly or maybe with a brand-new singer – where the band would take that melodic but hard-rocking sound of classic Sweet through the 1980s and give Queen a good run for their money. Sadly, things did not turn out that way.

'Big Apple Waltz' (Priest / Scott)

This is the affectionate ballad sung by Priest that was released as a single ahead of the UK album and reviewed above. A complete failure as a single, it certainly works better as an album track. However, to my mind, Sweet ballads always work best when they serve to provide some light and shade to the hard-rocking bombast of Sweet in full flow – just as 'Laura Lee' did on *Off The Record*. Sadly, there is not quite enough of that to really make the track stand out on this album.

'Dorian Gray' (Priest / Scott / Tucker)

Inspired by Oscar Wilde's ever-youthful portrait-owner, it tells the tale of an ageing female Hollywood star with a penchant for younger lovers. A jaunty pop-rock number, this would appear to provide something of a template for the tone of the next *Water's Edge* album, albeit without the additional complexity of Geoff Westley's arrangements, whose time with the band came to an end with this album. It is also noteworthy for being one of the two tracks on *Cut Above The Rest* where Tucker makes his debut on lead vocals.

'Discophony' (Dis-Kof-O-Ne) (Priest / Scott / Tucker / Moberly)

After the execrable 'Funk It Up' back in 1977, Sweet at last come up with a song about disco music whose sentiments I can really get behind. For a devoted rock fan, the lyrics are a glorious jibe at a music scene that was ubiquitous by the late 1970s:

Can't stand that disco music
Pain in my head
Everyone said
Disco is dead

In the US, Capitol released a single that doubled up 'Mother Earth' with 'Discophony', with the latter becoming popular with many rock DJs. 'Discophony' is certainly not completely free of the influence of the genre it seeks to satirise. Unlike 'Funk It Up', however, the song is very much a rock track with disco elements rather than a disco track performed by a rock band. The band's guest keyboard player, Gary Moberly, gets a co-writing credit on this one and would go on to get a couple more on the next album. It was actually Eddie Hardin (who was Steve Winwood's replacement in the Spencer Davis Group in the late 1960s) who came into the studio to provide the track's eerily distinctive synthesiser solo on an ARP2600, however.

'Eye Games' (Scott / Austin)
This is another song that emerged from the Clearwell writing sessions. A purely acoustic tune, the overall feel of the track is not unlike some of the material on the previous *Level Headed* album, although this time, the subject matter is about flirting and dating rituals in bars and nightclubs rather than magical fountains or ladies in lakes. While the song emanated from a tune written by Scott, the band's sound engineer, Louis Austin, also gets a co-writing credit, although it turns out that his wife, rather than Austin himself, may have been the one who assisted with the lyrics. This is the second song on the album where Tucker gets a lead vocal credit.

'Mother Earth' (Priest / Scott)
Written by Priest and Scott and with joint lead vocals from both, this is the most obvious prog-oriented track on the album. An extended piece of musical complexity with virtuoso instrumental passages, obvious parallels can be drawn with 'Love Is Like Oxygen' on the previous album. Unlike the latter, however, rather than being triumphant and majestic, the mood is far more introspective. It was never going to have the commercial appeal of 'Oxygen', and although it was released as a single in the US (doubled up with Discophony) it was never going to be a serious contender for a chart hit. However, it does show Sweet at their most experimental and ambitious and is one of the highlights on the album.

'Hold Me' (Scott)

Another slow romantic ballad, it is nowhere near as good as 'Big Apple Waltz' and to be truthful, it is probably one slow romantic ballad on the album too many. This one reflects on the breakdown of an old relationship rather than the excitement and intensity of a new one, and the morose tone of the lyrics is reflected in the music. Written and sung by Scott alone, this song never really seems to go anywhere yet at the same time appears to go on and on, just at a point when the album would have benefited from a more uplifting hard rock track.

'Stay With Me' (Priest / Scott / Tucker)

The original album ends with a slice of synth and guitar-dominated soft rock in the form of 'Stay With Me'. This began life with the working title of 'Log One' and then evolved into 'That Girl', one of the two songs that Connolly laid down before he was fired. It was finally re-written, re-titled and re-recorded with Priest on vocals. Scott writes in the liner notes for *Platinum Rare* when the original Connolly version finally saw the light of day, 'We spent a long time on this song and just about everything changed before it was finally released.' I am going to stick my neck out and say I much prefer the Connolly original rather than the version that appeared on the album, even if it did take him a week to nail the vocal.

While *Billboard* magazine and others in the US had given *Cut Above The Rest* fairly positive reviews, in the UK's weekly music papers, the knives were well and truly out. In *Record Mirror* reviewer Peter Coyne wrote, 'Sweet were the poppiest band of their time and a lot of fun then, but now they want to spoil the fun by growing up and playing... 'adult' rock.'

Sales-wise, the album also well and truly failed to put Sweet back on the map. Once again, it failed to make the UK album charts, but this had become almost an annual tradition – even at the height of the band's popularity. However, even in the band's most devoted market, it only managed to reach no. 49, the lowest ranking for a new Sweet studio album in the German album charts since *Funny How Sweet Co-Co Can Be* was released back in 1971. Over in the US, meanwhile, the album had spluttered to no. 151 in the Billboard charts when it was released earlier in the year.

None of this boded well for the release of *Water's Edge* the following year. Mike Chapman, still smarting from the way Sweet had severed links with their management-cum-songwriting duo and now enjoying a second creative wind with successful US New Wave acts like Blondie and The Knack, did not hesitate to stick the boot in. 'I don't think it makes me very happy to look back at the deaths of people like Mud and Sweet. A group dies; they're dead, gone and buried. Now they can't make a hit to save their lives,' he told *Melody Maker's* Harry Doherty in December 1979.

As both the year and the decade were about to draw to a close, however, few could have predicted the tragic situation that would unfold. On Boxing Day 1979, Tucker returned from a trip to his local pub to discover the lifeless body of his wife, Pauline, in the bathroom after she had fallen asleep in the bath.

On top of the official departure of the band's lead singer, two flop singles, a flop album, the further fracturing of the band with Priest's permanent relocation to the United States and a £500,000 tax bill, it was a sad and tragic finish to what had already been a catastrophic year for Sweet by anyone's reckoning.

Chapter Twelve: What Happened Next

The early 1980s would see the original band record two more studio albums as a three-piece, release a couple of singles and embark on one last UK tour before calling it a day.

Single Release
'Give The Lady Some Respect' (McRiner) b/w 'Tall Girls' (Priest / Scott / Tucker)
Personnel:
Steve Priest: bass guitar, vocals
Andy Scott: guitars, synthesisers, vocals
Mick Tucker: drums, vocals
Additional personnel:
Gary Moberly: piano, organ, synthesisers
Produced at Eastern Sound, Toronto, Kingsway Recorders, London and Marquee Studios, London, 1979 by Pip Williams and b/w by Sweet
UK release date: April 1980
Highest chart places: Did not chart

Written by Ray McRiner, who had toured with the band as an additional guitarist during the US tour in the summer of 1979, 'Give The Lady Some Respect' was Sweet's first single of the new decade. While McRiner was no longer working with the band by the time they entered the studio, some of his song ideas were put forward for consideration by dint of him sharing the same management as Sweet. One of the tracks pulled off the forthcoming *Water's Edge* album; the beginning rather gives the impression of an updated early 1980s take on a 1950s rock 'n' roll standard, particularly the jaunty riff and Priest's retro-sounding vocal. But the song promises more than it delivers and settles down into a fairly anodyne piece of pop-rock that lacks an irresistible hook.

The B-side 'Tall Girls' was a non-album, band-composed track on the theme of fellatio. Lyrically, it sounds like that the sort of smut the band excelled in at the time they were writing *Give Us A Wink*. While much rockier and more characteristically Sweet-sounding than the A-side, it does not have much of a melody and comes across more like the throwaway product of a studio jam rather than a carefully crafted piece of songwriting. From a band that were once masters of the unforgettable B-side, the track is something of a disappointment. The single sank without trace and failed to register a chart position anywhere.

Album Release
Water's Edge

Personnel:

Steve Priest: bass guitar, harmonica, vocals

Andy Scott: guitars synthesisers, vocals

Mick Tucker: drums, vocals

Additional personnel:

Gary Moberly: piano, organ, synthesisers

Produced at Eastern Sound, Toronto, Kingsway Recorders, London and Marquee Studios, London, 1979 by Pip Williams (tracks 1 and 10) and Sweet (all other tracks)

UK release date: August 1980

Highest chart places: Did not chart

Running time: 36:12

Tracks listing: 1. Sixties Man (Williams / Hutchins) 2. Getting In The Mood For Love (Priest / Scott / Tucker) 3. Tell The Truth (Priest / Scott / Moberly) 4. Own Up (Priest / Scott / Tucker) 5. Too Much Talking (McRiner) 6. Thank You For Loving Me (Scott / Moberly) 7. At Midnight (Scott) 8. Water's Edge (Priest / Scott / Tucker) 9. Hot Shot Gambler (Priest) 10. Give The Lady Some Respect (McRiner)

Opening with the now rather dated-sounding percussive synth that signals the beginning of 'Sixties Man', it pretty much sets the tone for the whole album. Generally considered to be the weakest Sweet album since *Funny How Sweet Co-Co Can Be* back in 1971, *Water's Edge* continues in the synth and guitar-based soft rock approach of *Cut Above The Rest*. However, whereas *Cut Above The Rest* was ambitious and experimental, with epic work-outs like 'Discophony' and 'Mother Earth', *Water's Edge* was a safe and fairly insipid serving of pop-rock. There is nothing absolutely ghastly on the album, but it lacks the innovation of its predecessor and there is an over-reliance on external material. Peter Hutchins and Pip Williams provided one of the songs while Ray McRiner provided two. Priest was clear in alleging that the choice of external songwriters was simply about Sweet manager, David Walker, getting a slice of publishing income through using artists that were already on his books. However, it must also be said that the band did enter the studio with a paucity of self-written material. Moreover, two of the tracks are overseen by an external producer for the first time since the band severed links with Mike Chapman and Nicky Chinn and in a supreme irony, said producer is none other than Pip Williams, who was one of the session players from the early days when the band were not even allowed to play on their own hits. Although it remains a better album overall and more satisfying listen than their 1971 debut, one cannot help feeling that things have started to come full circle for the band.

With a strangely literal cover showing the band appearing on a portable TV set with waves lapping around it and a wonky skyline in the background, the album chalked up positions in the lower reaches of the charts in a handful of places but sales were far from encouraging. In the US and Canada, the album was released with a completely different cover and retitled *VI* with a slightly re-ordered track-listing. It would be the band's sixth and final album for Capitol in the US.

Single Release
'Sixties Man' (Hutchins / Williams) b/w **'Oh Yeah'** (Priest / Scott / Tucker)

Personnel:
Steve Priest: bass guitar, vocals
Andy Scott: guitars, synthesisers, vocals
Mick Tucker: drums, vocals
Additional personnel:
Gary Moberly: piano, organ, synthesisers
Produced at Eastern Sound, Toronto, Kingsway Recorders, London and Marquee Studios, London, 1979 by Pip Williams b/w by Sweet
UK release date: October 1980
Highest chart places: Did not chart

Following the lack of success with *Water's Edge*, Polydor went on to release 'Sixties Man' as a single, which was the other Pip Williams-produced track from the album. On some versions, this was backed by 'Tall Girls', presumably Polydor deciding that so few people had got to hear the song when the previous single was released that they could recycle it without anyone noticing. In Germany, however, it was released with another non-album track, 'Oh Yeah' as the B-side. Like 'Tall Girls', it is rockier than the A-side but again lacks a memorable melody and comes across more like a studio jam. Like its predecessor, it failed to make any impact on the charts.

By the time 'Sixties Man' had been released, the band had reconvened to begin putting together tracks for another album. This would become the original band's final studio album: *Identity Crisis*. Arrangements were also put in place to play a one-off gig at London's Lyceum on 4 January 1981. This was to be the first UK concert the band had played since Hammersmith three years previously. While there was some trepidation within the band about the reaction they might receive, the show was a complete sell-out. The set-list was light on Chinn-Chapman hits (with only 'Ballroom Blitz' from the band's glam years) and heavy on self-penned singles, classic album tracks and B-sides, with a handful of songs from the forthcoming album thrown in, too. The crowd response was hugely enthusiastic and a nine-date UK tour that March was hurriedly arranged.

Rather than it being the start of a renaissance for the original band, however, it was to be a last hurrah. The Priest-Scott-Tucker line-up of Sweet played their last ever gig at Glasgow University on 21 March 1981. The band that had been formed back in 1968 was no more. It was ironic, really, that just as things finally fizzled out for Sweet, their old chart rivals, Slade, were enjoying something of a major revival. Having been a surprise success at Donington the previous year, filling in for a slot vacated by Ozzy Osbourne at the eleventh hour, Slade were now back in the UK top ten for the first time in years, enjoying support from fans of the growing New Wave Of British Heavy Metal movement. Indeed, a number of new UK heavy metal bands were citing Slade and Sweet as key influences. Newcastle band Raven, would cover two Sweet songs on their debut album released later that year, for example. While Slade were reaping the benefits, however, Sweet were winding down. Scott said in an interview with author in 2019: 'When the tour finished at the end of March '81 – I think it was Glasgow University – we never heard from Steve for ages. Mick had a tragedy. His first wife died ... Well, you wouldn't wish that on anybody, would you? And so he didn't want to do anything. And I was still out there – producing and writing and playing on other people's records.'

There was, however, still that final studio album to come out, albeit with an extremely limited release at the time.

Album Release
Identity Crisis
Personnel:
Steve Priest: bass guitar, lead vocals, backing vocals
Andy Scott: guitars, co-lead vocals (track 5), backing vocals
Mick Tucker: drums, backing vocals
Produced at Marcus Music Studios, London, 1980 by Sweet
UK release date: Not originally released in UK (released in Germany, November 1982)
Highest chart places: Did not chart
Running time: 33:41
Tracks listing: 1. Identity Crisis (Priest / Scott / Tucker) 2. New Shoes (Priest / Scott /

Tucker) 3. Two into One (Priest / Scott / Tucker) 4. Love Is The Cure (Scott) 5. It Makes Me Wonder (Priest / Scott / Tucker) 6. Hey Mama (Priest / Scott / Tucker) 7. Falling in Love (Priest / Scott / Tucker) 8. I Wish You Would (Arnold) 9. Strange Girl (Priest / Scott / Tucker)

Following the disappointing *Water's Edge* released in 1980, Sweet bounced back with a far stronger album, the prophetically-named *Identity Crisis* in 1982. The synth-driven pop-rock is out, the guitars are turned up, the sound is much meatier and the material far stronger. 'We're gonna forget the corn and blatant commerciality and get something a bit rawer,' Scott told *Sounds* in 1981. The trio deliver on that promise. As one would expect from a band like Sweet, the album is polished rather than gritty, but it is very much a rock album rather than an attempt at pop commerciality. In many ways it could be viewed as a natural successor to 1977's *Off The Record*, rather than the previous three albums. All of the songs are self-composed, bar one cover, which is the band's take on Billy Boy Arnold's Chicago blues standard 'I Wish You Would'. Although it obviously lacks the magic touch of their golden-haired singer from the band's heyday, Priest ably handles the bulk of the lead vocals and the trademark harmonies are still very much in evidence. From Scott's excellent lead guitar work-out on the title track to the catchy 'Love Is The Cure' to the classic, driving hard rock of 'Falling In Love', there is plenty to like on this album.

For the front cover, the band are photographed on stage in leather-clad 'rock god' mode, superimposed over an image of an eerily illuminated facial sculpture. No portable TV sets on the beach here. It would be nice to say that Sweet regained some momentum with this release, but, sadly, the band had finally split by the time it reached the shops – and the shops it did reach were few and far between. The album was released in Germany and Latin America, but the band's Capitol contract had come to an end, so it was not released in the US. Moreover, the album was not even given an official release in the band's home country and the remaining hard-core British Sweet fans had to track it down on import.

Even with a limited release, it is rather gratifying, however, that *Water's Edge* was not destined to be the final Sweet album from the original band and that the remaining trio left us with something far, far more satisfying. Unlike its predecessor, *Identity Crisis* is the kind of album that leaves one wanting more. It certainly left me wanting more at the time when I forked out significantly over the odds for it to obtain it on import as a sixteen-year-old teenager. Fortunately, in various formations, Sweet would be back in some form or another to give us more music a few years down the line.

It was, of course, a crying shame that Sweet sat out the early to mid-1980s, a time when the New Wave Of British Heavy Metal had given the UK hard rock scene a much-needed shot in the arm; when the US glam metal bands were taking off and when former 1970s glam acts like Slade, and even Gary Glitter, were back in the charts. And it was not just the British heavy metal and US hair metal scenes that had a glam infatuation, either. The early 1980s New Romantic scene would also lay claim to being a descendant of glam rock, even if their artistic pretensions and their Bowie-wannabe vocals most definitely put them at the 'high glam' end and their synths and drum machines were never going to match the energy of Sweet and Slade in full flow. The slightly later goth/alternative scene also took something from glam. Bauhaus certainly demonstrated a love for the genre. Peter Murphy of Bauhaus said in intlmusicsnobs.com in 2012: 'I always thought of Bauhaus as the Velvets gone holy, or the Sweet with better haircuts.'

Even with no official band out there, the British public were clearly still feeling some affection for Sweet. In September 1984, *Sweet 16*, a sixteen-track compilation, reached no. 49 in the UK album charts, the first time a Sweet album had been in the UK charts since *Sweet Fanny Adams* back in 1974. This was followed by a single 'It's It's... The Sweet Mix' which was a medley of 'Blockbuster!', 'Teenage Rampage', 'Hell Raiser' and 'Ballroom Blitz' and reached the top 50 in early 1985. Another medley single, 'The Wig Wam-Willy Mix', which brought together the earlier hits, reached no. 85 a few months later.

It was not long before Scott and Tucker were moved to reform Sweet. Scott told the author in 2019: 'So for a couple of years – '83-'84 – I was releasing some solo singles. And then in '85 – well at the end of '84 – I bumped into our old agent and he was looking after us in '81. And he said, 'Oh, I've got a bone to pick with you. I keep getting loads of enquiries. Are you still working with the Sweet?''

Things soon fell into place. Scott was back working with Tucker. A new vocalist, Paul Mario Day (who had been in an early line-up of Iron Maiden and then sang with another NWOBHM-era band called More), was recruited, along with keyboard player Phil Lanzon (who had previously been with Grand Prix). The nascent group began rehearsing with a temporary bass player while waiting for Priest, who had initially expressed interest in being part of the project, to fly out to join them. When Priest eventually declined to take part, that temporary bass player, Mal McNulty, was offered the job permanently.

Scott: 'I managed to get Mick out of retirement. Steve was even at least saying the right things, but Mick said, 'He's not coming back,' so luckily, I rehearsed a bass player. The guy who ended up in Sweet was actually Mal McNulty. We were using him to rehearse and I said he may not be coming, and he said, 'You're a mate of mine. I love this'. And, of course, we went to Australia with Mal and the rest is history'.

The new line-up bounced back with a live album recorded at London's historic Marquee Club in 1986. Paradoxically, two of the people in the Marquee Club audience were original Sweet members, Brian Connolly and Frank Torpey.

Torpey, interviewed at thesweetweb.com in 2018: 'As I walked in the club I could see this little fella with blonde hair and two girls with him. It slowly dawned on me this was Brian; as I walked behind him, I said 'Brian!' He turned around and said 'Torpey!!!' My god, you do look well. We got chatting at the bar and was amazed to hear he was no longer in the band; not only that, Stevie wasn't either. The band struck up with 'Action', we heard a few more numbers, but there was no point in me staying to say hi, as the only guy in the band I knew was Mick'.

As well as gigs in the UK, there were tours of mainland Europe and Australia and the renewed interest in Sweet then prompted an attempt by Mike Chapman to get all four members of the classic 1970s line-up working together once more. Studio time was booked in LA and in 1988, the three UK-based musicians flew out to join Priest in the US. Chapman, in an interview in *The Guardian* in 2010, said: 'I met them at the airport and Andy and Mick came off the plane. I said, 'Where's Brian?' They said, 'Oh, he's coming.' All of the people were coming off the plane by now. Then this little old man hobbled towards us. He was shaking and had a ghostly white face. I thought, 'Oh Jesus Christ.' It was horrifying.'

The sessions were soon abandoned. It is possible to hear some of the results on YouTube, which, sadly, show exactly why the sessions were rapidly abandoned. Priest, Scott and Tucker are all on fine form as they blast out some of Sweet's classics with renewed energy. To hear Connolly struggling through, his voice completely shot, is nothing short of a tragedy, however.

Two years later, all four members of the classic line-up would reconvene once more for a signing session and press conference at London's Tower Records to promote a new Sweet video compilation. 'There's got to be a demand for something, and I think that the time has never been better for us to think about getting ourselves back together and making some new records and getting out on the road,' Scott told an interviewer from

Capital Radio. It all came to nought, however. Priest returned to the States, Connolly continued performing with his own version of Sweet, and Scott and Tucker carried on with the reformed Sweet that they had established five years previously.

Tucker would eventually bow out in 1991, leaving Scott at the helm. Scott told thesweetweb.com in 2018: 'In the early '90s, he had a dramatic incident on a tour. I had to get a drummer to complete the tour. He wasn't exactly overly happy about that, but his wife immediately saw that he was in no state to be continuing. Within a year of that, he'd been diagnosed with pancreatitis and epilepsy. Within another couple of years of that, the leukaemia was diagnosed. I just remember thinking to myself, I wonder whether all of this is related to the incident in the early '90s.'

Tucker was replaced, initially, by Bodo Schopf and then shortly afterwards by Bruce Bisland – who remains with the band to this day. A number of albums have been released by Scott's version of Sweet over the years, often live recordings or studio re-recordings of old material. However, there have been albums of new material, too. These include '*A*' released in 1992, *Sweetlife* in 2002 and the covers album *New York Connection* in 2012. With various changes in personnel along the way, Scott's rebooted version of Sweet has continued to tour and record, delighting fans with classic Sweet songs. Scott: 'We've had a few people come and go, but when you look back over thirty-odd, almost forty years of reformation when you say you've had six singers that doesn't sound too bad really does it?'

Connolly, meanwhile, continued throughout the 1980s and the early to mid-1990s with his own career. After severing links with Sweet in 1978, he released two solo singles in 1980 for Polydor and a third in 1982 for Carrere. The first 'Take Away The Music' stayed true to Connolly's stated desire to explore country music on leaving Sweet, while the second 'Don't You Know A Lady' is uninspired late 1970s/early 1980s pop with a disco beat. The Carrere single 'Hypnotised' was by far the strongest of the three and could have put Connolly in contention as a solo rock performer, but sales were poor, and before long, he had reverted to using the Sweet name, firstly as the New Sweet and then as Brian Connolly's Sweet. The three solo singles, corresponding B-sides and assorted unreleased material were finally released as a compilation album *Take Away The Music* in 2004.

However, while Connolly's vocals on his three solo singles were perfectly creditable, his next release, an album of recordings of old Sweet songs which was put out as *Brian Connolly and The Sweet – Greatest*

Hits in 1986 was almost as tragic as the abandoned reunion sessions in LA two years later. A further album released in 1995 as *Brian Connolly's Sweet – Let's Go,* which combined re-recordings of Sweet material with three new songs, was significantly better, but there was no disguising the evident wear and tear on Connolly's voice. Things reached a nadir in November 1996 when Channel 4 screened a documentary *Don't Leave Me This Way* chronicling Connolly's attempts to keep the Sweet flame alive. A clearly ill Connolly is seen shaking profusely as he talks to the interviewer about surviving multiple heart attacks and is then seen struggling his way through the crowds to perform at a Butlins holiday camp. The documentary proved highly uncomfortable viewing for many Sweet fans and just a few months later, Connolly was dead. He had been hospitalised following a further heart attack and died in February 1997 following multiple heart problems, kidney failure and liver failure, aged just 51. Although they had had their differences in the past, Scott paid a fulsome and heartfelt tribute: 'Everyone's image of the Sweet was Brian – it was what he was put on this Earth for. I'll miss him.'

Obituaries at the time, while celebrating the achievements of the golden-haired singer who sang 'Blockbuster!', also dwelt on the tragic images from the recent documentary. This UK national newspaper obituary, from The Independent in 1997, was not untypical:

Don't Leave Me This Way, a Channel 4 documentary, highlighted the plight of Brian Connolly, who had suffered several heart attacks in 1981. Still clinging to his memorabilia and his dyed blond hair, the vocalist appeared as a shadow of his former self, shaking constantly and walking with a limp. He only came to life when appearing on stage at Butlin's to sing 'Blockbuster'.

Connolly's death was followed by Tucker's just five years later from leukaemia. Tucker had undergone a successful bone marrow transplant several years previously but finally succumbed to the disease after a series of recurring infections. He died in hospital in February 2002, aged 54. Scott, once more, paid a heartfelt tribute to a former bandmate: 'Mick Tucker was the best drummer around in the '70s. I played in the same band as him and was proud to do so. I feel extreme sadness, therefore that he has now left us and my heart goes out to Janet and Ayston with their sad loss. Miss you Mick – and then there were two.'

There was now just Scott and Priest left from the classic foursome. While Scott had busied himself with endless tours and several albums, Priest had maintained a relatively low profile in the years that followed the break-up of the original band. Permanently based in the US with his American wife Maureen, he initially spent time in New York, where he attempted to set up a band called the Allies with guitarist/vocalist Marco Delmar and drummer Steve Missal. Things never quite got off the ground and the project soon foundered. However, one of their compositions, 'Talk To Me', did end up featuring in a film called *Fast Food* recorded by the Rhythm Team. Priest and his wife then relocated to Los Angeles, where he wrote his autobiography *Are You Ready Steve?* Self-published in the 1990s, it goes into many detailed accounts of the bass player's musical and sexual adventures during his time in Sweet. 'I love the book, even if sometimes it reads like a Penthouse Forum. I laughed and cried too. Always entertaining,' was the pithy assessment of one fan on social media. After releasing a solo album *Priest's Precious Poems* in 2006, Priest finally formed his own version of Sweet in 2008, releasing one album featuring live recordings of various Sweet classics from a 2008 US concert. Following a short illness that had hospitalised him, Priest sadly passed away in June 2020.

When Connolly's death was announced back in 1997, it seemed like there were as many references to the tragic Channel 4 documentary as there were to his many musical achievements in Sweet's glory days. Meanwhile, when Tucker's death was announced in 2002, tributes were paid to his prolific talents as a drummer, but away from the dedicated Sweet fan-base, neither death particularly prompted any kind of wave of nostalgia for The Sweet or result in a stream of articles celebrating the cultural impact of 1970s glam rock. Priest's death, however, led to a global outpouring of affection, for the man, for the band and for their music. In an emphatically heartfelt tribute, Alexis Petridis for *The Guardian* lambasted those who only saw fit to lavish praise on the 'high glam' end of glam rock, populated by the likes of Bolan, Bowie and Roxy Music, while snootily dismissing those at the 'low glam' end as mere opportunists. 'No band personified low glam like The Sweet,' he wrote. 'And no member of The Sweet embodied low glam like bassist Steve Priest.'

Although Scott was the last of the classic line-up to join the original band, Priest's death left him as the last man standing. 'Then there was one!' he wrote on his band's Facebook page in the aftermath of Priest's death before launching into his own heartfelt, emotional and sincere tribute to his former bandmate: 'He was the best bass player I ever played with. The noise we made as a band was so powerful. From that moment in the summer of 1970 when we set off on our Musical Odyssey the world opened up and the rollercoaster ride started!'

Bibliography

Books
Auslander, P., *Performing Glam Rock – Gender and Theatricality In Popular Music* (University of Michigan Press, 2006)
Charlesworth, C., *Slade: Feel The Noize – An Illustrated Biography* (Omnibus Press, 1984)
Checksfield, P., *Look Wot They Dun – The Ultimate Guide to UK Glam Rock on TV in the 70s* (Self-published, 2019)
Cooper, K., Smay, D., *Bubblegum Music is the Naked Truth* (Feral House, 2001)
Duthie, M., *The Sweet – No Matter What They Say* (Self-published eBook, 2018)
Grundy, S., Tobler, J., *The Record Producers* (St. Martin's Press, 1983)
Logan, L., Woffinden, B., *The NME Book of Rock 2* (Wyndham Publications, 1977)
Priest, S., *Are You Ready Steve* (Self-published eBook, 2009)
Reynolds, R., *Shock and Awe – Glam Rock and its Legacy* (Faber & Faber, 2016)
Thompson, B., *Ban This Filth!: Letters from the Mary Whitehouse Archive* (Faber & Faber, 2012).
Thompson, D., *Blockbuster! – The True Story of The Sweet* (Cherry Red Books, 2010)
Trynka, P., *Starman – David Bowie: The Definitive Biography* (Sphere, 2011)
Turner, A.W., Glam Rock – *Dandies In The Underworld* (V & A Publishing, 2013)
Various, *Glam: The Genuine Article – Interviews Reviews Rare Photos* (NME Originals, 2004)
Weird & Gilly, *Mick Ronson – The Spider With The Platinum Hair* (Independent Music Press, 2009)

Magazine, Newspaper and Journal Articles
Barnes, K., 'Sweet: Glitter Relics in America', Phonograph Record, Oct, 1975
Barnes, K., 'The Glitter Era: Teenage Rampage', Bomp!, Mar, 1978
Bell, M., 'The Sweet: No Longer Unfashionable', NME, Apr, 1975
Cavanagh, D., 'Glam rock bottom: why did it go sour for Sweet?', Guardian, Sep, 2010
Charone, B., 'Give Us A Wink', Sounds, Feb, 1976

Crowe, C., 'The Sweet's Blitz of Hitz: 'They Were All Crap'', Rolling Stone, Dec, 1975

Doherty, H., 'Mike Chapman and Nicky Chinn: Ballroom Blitz & Hearts of Glass', Melody Maker, Dec, 1979

Dome, M., 'When Sweet went prog', Prog Magazine, Apr, 2019

Edmonds, B., 'The Sweet: Give Us A Wink', Phonograph Record, Mar, 1976

Fox-Cumming, R., 'Sweet Talking Guy', Disc, Feb, 1973

Fox-Cumming, R., 'Sweet, Geordie: Rainbow Theatre, London', Disc, Apr, 1973

Fox-Cumming, R., 'The Sweet smell of success turns to Mud in the eye', Disc, Feb, 1974

Frith, S., 'Sweet Notes', Creem, Nov, 1973

Goldman, V., 'Sweet: Sounds Girls in Sweet Nude Bathing Horror', Sounds, Jun, 1976

Goldstein, T., 'Sweet: Off The Record', Crawdaddy, Jul, 1977

Hull, R.A., 'Sweet: Desolation Boulevard', Creem, Aug, 1975

Ingham, J., 'Nicky Chinn and Mike Chapman: The Dynamic Duo of Plastic Pop', NME, Jun, 1973

Johnson, J., 'Sweet: Queens of the Hop', NME, Sept, 1973

Kent, N., 'The Sweet Soft Underbelly of Rock', NME, Feb, 1973

Ling, D., 'The Sweet: Is it finally time to give them the credit they deserve?', Classic Rock, Oct, 2017

Nooger, D., 'Sweet But Not Saccharine', Circus, Mar, 1976

Perrone, P., 'Obituary: Brian Connolly', Independent, Feb, 1977

Petridis, A., 'Steve Priest: the outrageous Sweet bassist who presaged heavy metal', Guardian, Jun, 2020

Plummer, M., 'We're tired of being dismissed as a teenybop band say the Wig Wam Bam men', Melody Maker, Jan, 1972

Rees, J., 'Does anyone know the way to blockbuster?', The Arts Desk, Jun, 2015

Reigel, R., 'Give Us A Wink', Creem, May, 1976

Ross, R., 'Sparks vs. Sweet: The Battle for Britain', Phonograph Record, Aug, 1974

Salewicz, C., 'The Sweet: Top of the Pops', NME, Jan, 1976

Shaar Murray, C., 'Sweet: Rainbow Theatre, London', NME, Apr, 1973

Shearlaw, J., 'Sweet: Level Headed' (album review), Record Mirror, Feb, 1978

Silverton, P., 'The Sweet: Sweet's Golden Greats' (album review), Sounds, Nov, 1977

Sperrazza, G., 'The Sweet: Sweet Fanny Adams', Shakin' Street Gazette, Sept, 1974

Sperrazza, G., 'Sweet: Desolation Boulevard'. Phonograph Record, Feb, 1975

Thomson, D., 'As Sweet As It Was', Goldmine, Feb, 1997

Tiven, J., 'The Sweet' (album review), Zoo World, Oct, 1973

Uncredited writer, 'Can You Take The Sweet Seriously', Beat Instrumental, Nov, 1973

Uncredited writer, 'Sweet more than a singles band', Disc, Apr, 1974

Uncredited writer, 'Sweet star follows brother Taggart to grave', Scottish Daily Record, Feb, 1997

Zarebski, J. 'Review: Expansions On Life – The Elastic Band', Record Collector, May, 2009

Online and digital resources

1037theloon.com Swanson, D., 'How Sweet finally broke out with Sweet Fanny Adams', Apr, 2015

Alwynturner.com 'Glitter Suits & Platform Boots'

Ballroom Hitz: The Very Best Of Sweet (VHS, PNE Video, 1996)

Darrensmusicblog.com (Author's interview with Andy Scott, Nov, 2019)

Davidbuckingham.net 'Glitter, glam and gender play: pop and teenybop in the early 1970s'

Glitz, Blitz & Hitz: The Very Best of Sweet (DVD, Weinerworld 2003)

rockhistorymusic.com (Video interviews with Andy Scott, Jan, 2021)

RPM45 (Podcast interview with Andy Scott, Jan, 2021)

Sweet – Action: The Ultimate Story (3-DVD Box set, Sony, 2015)

Thestrangebrew.co.uk (Warburton, N. 'Wainright's Gentlemen')

thesweetband.com (US Sweet website – Steve Priest)

thesweet.com (UK Sweet website – Andy Scott)

thesweetweb.com (Ragogna. M., Interview with Andy Scott)

thesweetweb.com (Interview with Frank Torpey)

Decades Series
Pink Floyd In The 1970s – Georg Purvis 978-1-78952-072-9
Marillion in the 1980s – Nathaniel Webb 978-1-78952-065-1

On Screen series
Carry On... – Stephen Lambe 978-1-78952-004-0
David Cronenberg – Patrick Chapman 978-1-78952-071-2
Doctor Who: The David Tennant Years – Jamie Hailstone 978-1-78952-066-8
Monty Python – Steve Pilkington 978-1-78952-047-7
Seinfeld Seasons 1 to 5 – Stephen Lambe 978-1-78952-012-5

Other Books
Derek Taylor: For Your Radioactive Children – Andrew Darlington
978-1-78952-
Jon Anderson and the Warriors - the road to Yes – David Watkinson
978-1-78952-059-0
Tommy Bolin: In and Out of Deep Purple – Laura Shenton
978-1-78952-070-5
Maximum Darkness – Deke Leonard 978-1-78952-048-4
Maybe I Should've Stayed In Bed – Deke Leonard 978-1-78952-053-8
The Twang Dynasty – Deke Leonard 978-1-78952-049-1

and many more to come!

Would you like to write for Sonicbond Publishing?

At Sonicbond Publishing we are always on the look-out for authors, particularly for our two main series:

On Track. Mixing fact with in depth analysis, the On Track series examines the work of a particular musical artist or group. All genres are considered from easy listening and jazz to 60s soul to 90s pop, via rock and metal.

On Screen. This series looks at the world of film and television. Subjects considered include directors, actors and writers, as well as entire television and film series. As with the On Track series, we balance fact with analysis.

While professional writing experience would, of course, be an advantage the most important qualification is to have real enthusiasm and knowledge of your subject. First-time authors are welcomed, but the ability to write well in English is essential.

Sonicbond Publishing has distribution throughout Europe and North America, and all books are also published in E-book form. Authors will be paid a royalty based on sales of their book.

Further details are available from www.sonicbondpublishing.co.uk. To contact us, complete the contact form there or email info@sonicbondpublishing.co.uk